CELTIC

PACKED WITH INFORMATION ON THE BHOYS

CELTIC

This edition published and distributed by Parragon, 1998

Parragon
Unit 13-17 Avonbridge Trading Estate
Atlantic Road
Avonmouth
Bristol BS11 9QD

Produced by Magpie Books,
an imprint of Robinson Publishing Ltd, London

ISBN 0 75252 548 4

A copy of the British Library Cataloguing-in-Publication
Data is available from the British Library.

Printed and bound in the EC.

This independent publication has been prepared without any
involvement on the part of Celtic Football Club or the
Scottish Premier League.

CELTIC

PACKED WITH INFORMATION ON THE BHOYS

Chris Mason

PARRAGON

CONTENTS

INTRODUCTION

Scottish football is dominated by the two Glasgow giants – and Celtic, the team in the green, have always considered themselves top dogs. They were first to bring home continental silverware when the European Cup was secured by the 'Lisbon Lions' in 1967, and set the pace at home under the great Jock Stein with a record nine Championship wins.

The legends that have graced the Parkhead pitch are many and various, ranging from Jimmy McGrory to Kenny Dalglish, while managers to rival the previously mentioned 'Big Man' include Willie Maley and former player Billy McNeill. There are more memories than any number of books could contain, and the story still continues under the stewardship of general manager Jock Brown (brother of national manager Craig) and coach Wim Jansen, who's already notched his first trophy.

By dividing Celtic's history into easily digestible sections, this book seeks to inform and entertain. It cannot by its very size be exhaustive, and it is hoped that anyone fascinated by the facts and figures will purchase one of the weighty club histories available or follows Celtic's match-by-match progress through the *Rothmans Football Yearbook*, published annually.

In these pages, however, you'll find details of the great players and double acts, the managers profiled together with their achievements, quotes, statistics, dream teams, month-by-month milestones…in short, much of what has gone to make this club a football institution.

GOALS GALORE!

Few football clubs can claim to have a large number of players, each of whom has scored more than a hundred goals in major competitions. Celtic, however, have 26 such strikers who, down the years, each scored more than the magic ton.

James Edward McGrory was a phenomenon. As a young player he was accused of having flat feet and was not considered to have great goalscoring potential, yet he went on to score an incredible 472 goals at an average of just over a goal per game.

Flat feet notwithstanding, McGrory became an accomplished header of the ball and was famed for an ability to direct headers towards goal with more ferocity than most players of his day could manage with their own perfectly normal feet. He started scoring soon after his League debut at the start of the 1924-25 season and achieved his first hat-trick in his eighth game, a 4-0 victory over Motherwell. He was in and out of the side during that first season but managed another hat-trick as well as scoring fours against Falkirk and Third Lanark. In October 1926 he hit five in a 6-2 win over Aberdeen and a few weeks later he repeated this performance as Dundee United went down 7-2.

McGrory really was a very remarkable goalscorer. A week before the Dundee United game he had netted four times in a 6-0 victory at Dunfermline and he went on to score a total of 56 goals in 39 League and Cup games during that 1926-27 season. More hat-tricks, as well as a few fours and fives, followed but McGrory went totally berserk during the following season when, once more, poor old Dunfermline were the victims. This time Celtic won 9-0, Jimmy scoring eight.

McGrory suffered a lot of knocks during his playing career, but for the most part he ignored them. He scored the only goal of the 1933 Cup Final against Motherwell, having sustained two broken teeth and a cut lip during the early stages, and by the time his career was over he was easily the most prolific goalscorer in the history of British football.

No one comes close to Jimmy McGrory when it comes to goalscoring, but Robert Lennox MBE certainly did his best. Born in Saltcoats in 1943, Lennox joined Celtic and was soon a member of the first-team squad. He scored in the 5-1 victory at Basle as Celtic embarked upon a European Cup Winners' Cup adventure in 1963, and during his career at Celtic Park he netted 273 times in 571 games even though, as Bobby himself said, his main job as an outside-left was to 'look for space and run'.

Lennox was a marvellous team man. He was always extremely fit and so fast that, on occasion, linesmen would flag when he had been onside, unable to believe that he had

	CELTIC'S TOP 10 SCORERS			
	Player	**From-To**	**Apps**	**Goals**
1	Jimmy McGrory	1922-37	445	472
2	Bobby Lennox	1961-80	571	273
3	Steve Chalmers	1959-71	405	228
4	Jimmy Quinn	1900-15	331	216
5	Patsy Gallagher	1911-26	464	196
6	John Hughes	1959-71	416	189
7	Sandy McMahon	1890-1903	217	171
8	Jimmy McMenemy	1902-20	515	168
9	Kenny Dalglish	1967-77	320	166
10	Adam McLean	1917-28	408	138

not been offside when the ball had been dispatched in his general direction. In 1965 he scored in every round played in the Scottish Cup competition except the Final, in which Celtic beat Dunfermline 3-2, and in the following season scored two in each of three successive League games against Aberdeen, Hearts and Falkirk respectively. During that season he also bagged a hat-trick at the home of remarkably named Dutch opponents Go Ahead in the European Cup Winners' Cup.

In 1967-68 Lennox netted four times in a 5-1 victory over Partick Thistle and again scored four when Celtic visited Perth and beat St Johnstone 6-1. Then, in 1968-69, Partick were on the receiving end once more, this time in the League Cup. Lennox scored five and, little more than a week later, scored another five in a 10-0 victory over Hamilton Academicals – the remaining nap hand being netted by Steve Chalmers. Lennox then waited until the Final before scoring a hat-trick in the 6-2 win over Hibernian.

Bobby Lennox made and scored many more goals during his career, as his club went on to greater domestic and European glory – helped by another great goal scorer, Steve Chalmers. Steve, born in Glasgow in December 1936, made 405 appearances in a Celtic shirt and scored 228 goals between 1959 and 1971. A quiet and unassuming man, he tended to score most of his goals in ones and twos but, in August 1964, he put three past Partick Thistle in a League Cup match and then, a month later, scored five against East Fife in the same competition.

But the best was yet to come. On 25 May 1967, he scored what must have been the most important goal of his career – the winner in the European Cup Final against Inter Milan, which was just reward for a fine display of attacking football. Another goal of which he is justly proud resulted from a solo run down the left wing against Rangers in the 1969 Scottish Cup Final – a game Celtic won 4-0.

Steve Chalmers' Celtic career was virtually ended by a broken leg sustained in the League Cup Final against St Johnstone in 1969.

Jimmy Quinn, Patsy Gallagher, John Hughes, Kenny Dalglish and many others all scored well over 100 goals in Celtic's famous green and white. And doubtless many more will do so in the future.

A FEW UNUSUAL LEAGUE SCORES				
5 May 1891	Celtic	9	Vale of Leven	1
26 October 1895	Celtic	11	Dundee	0
25 December 1897	Celtic	9	Clyde	1
11 November 1922	Celtic	1	Ayr Utd	4
10 January 1931	Celtic	9	East Fife	1
30 April 1937	Motherwell	8	Celtic	0
13 August 1938	Celtic	9	Kilmarnock	1
17 December 1949	East Fife	5	Celtic	1
22 December 1956	Airdrie	3	Celtic	7
27 March 1963	Kilmarnock	6	Celtic	0
14 April 1965	Falkirk	6	Celtic	2
4 September 1971	Celtic	9	Clyde	1
3 January 1987	Celtic	8	Hamilton	3
5 November 1988	Hamilton	0	Celtic	8
19 September 1992	Falkirk	4	Celtic	5

THROUGH THE YEARS
JANUARY

1892
January
23

Celtic played Cowlairs in the Quarter-Final of the Scottish Cup. They won 4–1, with goals from Alec Brady (2), John Madden and Sandy McMahon – and were on their way to capturing the Cup for the first time in their history.

1928
January
14

Jimmy McGrory, already known for great feats of goalscoring, netted three times in the first nine minutes of a League game against bottom club Dunfermline. Jimmy however was far from content with that, and went on to score a total of eight, setting a world record for the number of goals scored by one man in a single game.

1940
January
1

Willie Maley had been in charge at Celtic for an incredible 43 years, but he was 71 years old and the directors thought it was time for him to move over. Maley was not, it must be said, the easiest of men and he was in dispute with the club over a taxation arrangement. In addition, the directors were not keen on the fact that the Celtic players used a restaurant owned by the manager as a meeting place. Willie didn't want to go, but finally resigned on New Year's Day.

1963

January

5

Celtic beat Aberdeen 5–1 at Pittodrie, with a hat–trick from John Hughes and two more from Bobby Craig – who was playing the game of his life. Only four days earlier Celtic had gone down 4–0 at Ibrox, and prior to that Aberdeen had triumphed by two goals to one at Parkhead.

Almost exactly a year after the 5–1 defeat of Aberdeen, on 4 January 1964, Celtic beat Falkirk 7–0, while on 30 January 1965 Aberdeen were again beaten – Celtic this time putting eight past the Dons without reply, five of them coming from John Hughes. On 3 January 1966 Rangers were beaten 5–1 at Parkhead and, in the following season, both Dundee and Clyde were beaten by the same score in the same month.

1995

January

Following a great deal of upset and controversy, Fergus McCann finally got his share issue off the ground. The money raised enabled Celtic to complete the new stadium.

DREAM TEAM 1

Between 1905 and 1910 Celtic won
the Scottish League Championship six
years running. They also won the Scottish
Cup in 1907 and 1908, and might have
done so in 1909, had it not been for the
Hampden Riot.

14

Goalkeeper   **Davie Adams**

Much loved by the supporters of the day, Adams had also helped Celtic to win the Cup in 1904, and was ever-present in 1904–05, 1905–06 and 1907–08.

Right-back   **Donnie McLeod**

Also ever-present in the first season. McLeod was a fearless full-back who was to be killed during the Great War.

Left-back   **Jimmy Weir**

Weir, who held down the left flank of the defence from 1907–08, was to fall out of favour and leave for Middlesbrough in August 1910

Right-half   **Jim Young.**

Although born in Kilmarnock, 'Sunny Jim' was signed from Bristol Rovers in 1903 and remained with Celtic until 1917. He was a splendid tackler and did a great deal to engineer the club's early success.

Centre-half   **Willie Loney**

Loney was not particularly tall for a centre-half and sometimes played at outside-right. He was known as the Obliterator and he had a very fierce shot.

Left-half   **Jimmie Hay**

Another vigorous tackler who combined touch with strength in the centre of the park.

Outside-right   **Alec Bennett**

Bennett mainly occupied the Number 7 shirt until he did the unthinkable and moved to Rangers in May 1908. He scored 53 times in his 152 Celtic appearances,

Inside-right   **Jimmy McMenemy**

McMenemy scored on 168 occasions in his 515 games, had remarkable speed and was a great header of the ball. He served Celtic for almost two decades.

Centre-forward   **Jimmy Quinn**

Between 1904–05 and 1909–10, the great Jimmy Quinn scored 11 League hat-tricks as well as netting four times on two further occasions.

Inside-left   **Peter Somers**

Scorer of 62 goals for Celtic, Somers was also an accomplished pianist.

Outside-left   **Davie Hamilton**

Another very speedy player who, at times, gave a truly brilliant performance with the ball, although his crosses were inclined to be somewhat wayward.

APPEARANCES

In their 110-year history, Celtic have had more than three dozen players who have made more than 300 first-team appearances.

Towering central defender Billy McNeill appeared in almost 800 games between 1957 and 1975. By the beginning of the 1966–67 season he had virtually made the Number 5 shirt his own and was to remain its main occupier for the next eight seasons. He missed only one game in 1966–67 (playing in all nine European Cup matches) and was ever-present in 1967–68. The next season saw him miss only one League Cup game while 1969–70 saw him miss three – mind you, he did play in the other 56! Five games were missed in 1970–71, three in 1971–72, and just 20 in the next three seasons. It was an incredible record.

Stalwart defender-midfielder Roy Aitken was born in Irvine in November 1958. He joined Celtic in June 1975 and left for Newcastle in January 1990, playing for the Bhoys on 667 occasions. He helped his side win the Double in 1977, as well as the Championship in 1979, 1981, 1982 and 1986. He also won a Scottish Cup medal in 1980 and his cross enabled Frank McGarvey to head the winner against Dundee United in the Cup Final of 1985. He then captained his side to further glory, including the Centenary Year Double in 1988.

Aitken missed just one game in 1978–79 and only 22 in the next six seasons. He was then ever present in 1985–86 and missed no more than the odd game over the three subsequent campaigns. He was undoubtedly a Celtic stalwart – as, of course, was right-back Danny McGrain, who played 657 times for the club between 1967 and 1987. McGrain suffered many injuries during his long career but overcame them all to earn a testimonial game against Manchester United which attracted a crowd of 45,000.

Eire international goalkeeper Packy Bonner played in a couple of games during the 1978-79 season, but began to make an impact at the beginning of 1980-81. He was between the posts on the opening day of that season (9 August 1980) and missed only two games between then and October 1983. Injury caused him to miss some matches over the next few seasons but he remained the number one choice until shortly before an abortive free transfer to Kilmarnock in the summer of 1994 (the arrival new manager Tommy Burns quickly convinced him to change his mind). In all, he played in 632 first-team encounters and was most certainly one of Celtic's best ever goalkeepers.

Another modern-day player to have made a large number of appearances is Paul McStay. He made his debut in the Championship side of 1981-82 and between 1982-83 and 1994-95 was first choice for the Number 8 shirt. Altogether, he made a total of 676 first-team appearances before injury forced his retirement at a cruelly early age.

Delving further back in history, we find Alec McNair who played in 604 games between 1904-25. A natural right-back, he was born in Bo'ness in December 1883 and played for Stenhousemuir before joining the Celts. His career was affected by the First World War, but even so he won 12 Championship and five Cup winner's medals.

In the ten seasons between 1910-11 and the outbreak of hostilities, McNair missed an average of just four and a half games per campaign – a remarkable record for a defender. There were no ever-present seasons, but the right-back continued to give sterling service after the war and won his final Championship medal in 1922. When he finally retired from football, he became a stockbroker.

Bobby Lennox, Jimmy McMenemy and Jimmy Johnstone all made well over 500 appearances in the hoops. So, too, did Bobby Evans (1944–60) who was ever-present in 1954–55 and missed very few games during the following three seasons. Those having more than 400 to their credit include Tommy Burns, Bobby Murdoch, Jimmy McStay, Patsy Gallagher, Jimmy McGrory, Bertie Peacock, Alec Thomson, Charlie Shaw, Andy McAtee, Willie McStay, Tommy Gemmell, John Hughes, Adam McLean, Charlie Shaw and Steve Chalmers.

Sons follow fathers and wee brothers sometimes follow big ones. Here are some Celtic family connections:

• Paul Chalmers, son of the famous Steve, made just four appearances for Celtic. He moved to Swansea for a large fee and later won a Welsh Cup medal.

• Mike Conroy played in just eight matches between 1953 and 1960. His son, also named Mike, did rather better, making 89 appearances and scoring 14 goals between 1978 and 1982.

• Brothers James and John Devlin each made two Celtic appearances during the 1890s.

• John Divers played in 115 matches and scored 44 goals prior to World War Two. His son, John junior, made 232 appearances, scoring on 102 occasions, between 1957 and 1966. The younger Divers was also a grand nephew of Patsy Gallagher.

• Goalkeeper Mick Dolan played in four matches in the 1890s, keeping one clean sheet, while his brother Frank, a centre-half, played in just two.

• The Dunbar brothers, Mick and Tom, also played during the 19th century's last decade. Mick played on 32 occasions and scored ten times, while Tom, a right-back, made 60 appearances and scored four times.

• The great Patsy Gallagher had five sons. Willie, the eldest, signed for Celtic in 1938, made 39 appearances and scored five goals.

• Centre-half Willie Lyon had a younger brother called Tom, who played just three times for the club.

• The Maley brothers – also Willie and Tom – played during the 1890s. Willie played 96 times, while Tom made just nine appearances. The latter did however find the net on six occasions.

• Goalkeeper Gordon Marshall played in one Drybrough Cup game, in 1971. His only other appearance was in a first round European Cup tie versus Boldklub in Copenhagen a few weeks later, which Celtic lost 2-1. His son, who bears the marvellous name of Gordon George Banks Marshall, has done rather better.

• The great outside-right Andy McAtee had a nephew called Tony, who made four wartime appearances for Celtic.

• George McCluskey scored 78 goals in his 204 Celtic games. His younger brother John was not so lucky. Having shown tremendous promise, which led to a place on the subs' bench in a European Cup tie in September 1977, he was forced by a thrombosis to retire from the game at the age of 19.

• Tommy McInally who, as a centre-forward between 1919-22 and an inside-left between 1925-28, scored 127 goals in 213 Celtic appearances, caused a few problems during his spell at Parkhead. His brother Arthur made just one appearance as a centre-half.

• Jimmy McMenemy's 515 Celtic appearances were not matched by those of his brother John, who played just 16 times between 1925 and 1928.

• When John McPhail retired in 1956, having played 131 times for Celtic, his brother Billy joined the Celts. He made 57 appearances and scored 38 goals.

• Willie McStay (1977-78, 90 appearances) is the big brother of Paul McStay and the grand nephew of both Willie McStay (1912-1929, 446 appearances) and Jimmy McStay (1920-1934, 472 appearances).

THROUGH THE YEARS
FEBRUARY

1889
February
9

Celtic reached the Final of the Scottish Cup for the first time. On the way they had recorded some notable victories, including an 8-0 win over Cowlairs and a 9-2 victory over Clyde, but now they had to face the might of Third Lanark. As ever, conditions on the day were appalling at Hampden Park, and although Celtic lost 3-0 it was decided that the game should be replayed a week later. It was, and this time the Celts went down 2-1.

1905
February
9

Barney Battles was a defender who spent two periods at Parkhead between 1895 and 1905, making 136 appearances. He was total inspiration every game he played but sadly he died on 9 February after an attack of infuenza. His coffin was carried by four Celtic players, and it was followed by 2,000 people, with another 40,000 lining the route.

Celtic played four League games this month and scored 14 goals without conceding any. Their victims were Aberdeen (4-0 away), Dumbarton (6-0 at home), Queen's Park (1-0 away) and Dundee (3-0 at home).

The year's second month can prove difficult for football. During February 1963 Celtic, in common with a number of other sides, played no League or Cup matches due to adverse weather conditions.

In 1975 Celtic had signed a young player on schoolboy forms. He developed rather well and, as his family was already known, to the club the decision was made to offer him a full contract. His name was Paul Michael Lyons McStay.

GREAT STRIKERS

Parkhead's goalscoring gallery has contained a plethora of charismatic characters. Here are some past and present stars.

 ## JIMMY QUINN

By all accounts, Jimmy Quinn was a pretty hard man. He was born at Croy on 8 July 1878 and joined Celtic in the first year of the new century. He made his debut in a 4-3 win at St Mirren in January 1901, scoring one of Celtic's goals in what was an end–of–season fixture. He was in the side at the beginning of the following season and, in October, scored in a 2-2 draw with Rangers. Unfortunately, he also scored an own goal in this match.

Quinn was now an established member of the side but was not regularly on the scoresheet until 1904-05, when he netted a couple of hat-tricks. In March 1906 he scored four in a 6-0 win at Queen's Park, and he repeated this feat on the opening day of the 1908-09 season, in a 5-0 victory at Morton. Later that season he scored hat-tricks in two succesive League games, at home to Motherwell and at Queen's Park once more.

Jimmy Quinn had started off as a left-winger. After a game against Queen's Park in March 1901, one reporter wrote that 'Quinn played splendidly on the left, shooting and centring in a manner reminiscent of Johnny Campbell in his younger days', but it was at centre-forward that he really came into his own. Rangers were leading 2-0 in the Scottish Cup Final of 1904 when Quinn decided to take matters in hand. He scored one, and then another, before finally netting the winner just seven minutes from the end. Needless to say, his team mates went wild – and, no doubt, the Celtic fans were really quite pleased as well.

Quinn's 'questionable style of deportment' got him into trouble on more than one occasion, and he was ordered from the field several times and faced a number of lengthy suspensions. A Scottish international (11 caps), he played 331 games for Celtic and scored 216 goals. In all, he won six consecutive League Championship medals and witnessed his captain hold aloft the Scottish Cup on five occasions, before a knee injury forced him into retirement early in 1915. Described as a rampaging tiger of a centre-forward, this mighty Quinn died in his home town in November 1945.

JIMMY QUINN CELTIC RECORD 1900-15									
League		FA Cup		League Cup		Europe		Total	
Apps	Goals	Apps	Goals	Apps	Goals	Apps	Goals	Apps	Goals
273	187	58	29	—	—	—	—	331	216

 # JIMMY McGRORY

Jimmy McGrory was, quite simply, the most prolific goal scorer ever to play football in Britain. McGrory saw himself at inside-right but he was playing at outside-left when Celtic took an interest in him, and signed him in June 1921. Born in Garngad on 26 April 1904, he made his Celtic debut in a 1-0 defeat at Third Lanark in January 1923. He became a regular in the Number 9 shirt in season 1924-25 and missed just one game in 1925-26, a season in which he scored 42 League and Cup goals.

The goals continued to flow in subsequent seasons. In 1926-27 he scored five in a game on three occasions, four in a game on four occasions and another hat-trick for good measure. In 1927-28 he scored eight against Dunfermline, this being preceded by hat-tricks in the two previous League games. McGrory scored 47 League goals during that season, as well as six in the Scottish Cup, while as late as 1935-36, he scored in ten consecutive League matches (16 goals in all) while failing to score in only four of the 32 League games in which he played.

McGrory had 'shoulders like a young Clydesdale, neck like a prime Aberdeen Angus and a head the nightmare of every goalkeeper'. In view of his goalscoring achievements, it is a little surprising that manager Willie Maley considered transferring him to Herbert Chapman's Arsenal in 1928. McGrory would certainly have made more money at Highbury, but he was Celtic through and through and had no intention of moving south.

McGrory and Celtic won League Championship honours in 1925-26 and 1935-36 and also at the end of McGrory's last playing season, 1937-38, while the Scottish Cup was won in 1925 (Jimmy scored), 1927 (though Jimmy was missing from the Final), 1931 (Jimmy scored twice), 1933 (Jimmy scored the game's only goal) and 1937 (Jimmy failed to score!)

Jimmy McGrory played seven times for Scotland and notched up 472 goals in 445 Celtic games. He later returned to Parkhead as manager and died in Glasgow on 20 October 1982, aged 78.

JIMMY McGRORY CELTIC RECORD 1922-37									
League		FA Cup		League Cup		Europe		Total	
Apps	Goals	Apps	Goals	Apps	Goals	Apps	Goals	Apps	Goals
378	398	67	74	—	—	—	—	445	472

BOBBY LENNOX

Bobby Lennox, who was born in Saltcoats on 30 August 1943, gets more than a mention elsewhere in this book as he is one of Celtic's all-time leading goalscorers. He joined the club in September 1961 and, unlike his contemporary Jimmy Johnstone, he never gave his manager any trouble or cause for concern. He began as a straightforward outside-left but Stein wanted to use him in the inside-left position. 'He got me lying well upfield, ready for the whip through,' said Lennox. 'I was on the move, in fact, before the pass was made.'

His first game was a League encounter with Dundee in March 1962, which Celtic won 2-1, and his last on 2 May 1980 when he was a substitute for the Scottish Cup Final against Rangers, which Celtic won 1-0 in extra time. In-between times, he made 569 Celtic appearances – 66 of which were in European competitions – and scored a toal of 273 goals (13 in Europe). Celtic won 11 League Championships while Lennox was playing, as well as the European Cup. He also won five Scottish Cup winner's medals and four for winning the League Cup. In the 1968 League Cup Final Lennox scored a hat-trick as Celtic beat Hibernian 6-2.

Lennox also won ten Scottish caps, but his career was probably best summed up by Billy McNeill, when he said: 'Bobby Lennox knows what wearing a Celtic jersey means.'

BOBBY LENNOX CELTIC RECORD 1961-78, 1978-80									
League		FA Cup		League Cup		Europe		Total	
Apps	Goals	Apps	Goals	Apps	Goals	Apps	Goals	Apps	Goals
335	167	51	31	119	62	66	13	571	273

KENNY DALGLISH

Kenny Dalglish was born in Dalmarnock on 4 March 1951. He signed as a full professional for Celtic on 29 April 1968 and made his debut in a League Cup game at Hamilton Academicals in September of the same year. Sometimes described as a utility player, this hardly seems an apt description of a footballer who was undoubtedly one of the most instinctive players ever to put on a pair of boots.

When Jock Stein was asked just what was Dalglish's best position, he replied: 'Och, just let him out on the park.' In fact, Dalglish was that rare commodity – a player with virtually no weaknesses. He both made and scored goals, he defended brilliantly and, surprisingly for a player who put himself about so much, he suffered remarkably few injuries.

In 1977 he was captain of the Double (and very nearly Treble) winning side and most Celtic supporters believed that the team was once more good enough to rival the best Europe had to offer. But the hopes and dreams of many a Celt were to be dashed, as it was with Liverpool that Dalglish won the European Cup in 1978.

There was irony here, as Bill Shankly had turned Dalglish down as a 15-year-old, perhaps because he was small and would maybe lack stamina. Even Shanks got it wrong sometimes! Dalglish made 47 of his Scotland appearances while with Celtic, and of course went on to make many more.

While at Parkhead he won four League Championship medals, four Scottish Cup winner's medals and one medal for winning the League Cup. He joined Liverpool on 10 August 1977, having played 320 times for Celtic and having scored 166 goals. Jock Stein was not amused. At Anfield, however, Dalglish would add considerably to his medal tally.

KENNY DALGLISH CELTIC RECORD 1967-77									
League		**FA Cup**		**League Cup**		**Europe**		**Total**	
Apps	**Goals**	**Apps**	**Goals**	**Apps**	**Goals**	**Apps**	**Goals**	**Apps**	**Goals**
204	112	29	11	60	35	27	8	320	166

HENRIK LARSSON

At first sight, striker Henrik Larsson looks anything but Swedish with his dreadlocked hair trailing behind him. Yet he shot to fame in his native land with 16 goals in 1993, his first season with Helsingborg, and an international career that began as that season closed with a debut in a 3–2 win over neighbouring Finland. Playing and scoring in a World Cup qualifying game clearly held no fears for the youngster, and, just as Sweden booked their place in the Finals, he too was on his way to great things – a berth at Feyenoord.

His first season in Dutch football was a relatively quiet one, and he found his place in the national starting line-up far from guaranteed. Yet he made a big impact when he did play, often emerging from the substitute's bench to turn games with his pace and close control. This paid off when he was selected against Bulgaria in a play-off match in Los Angeles and ended the tournament with a fine individual goal.

Wim Jansen was clearly well aware of Larsson's talents, as was Dutch football in general, and swooped to make him one of his first signings when appointed to the Parkhead hotseat. Since then, the player has linked well with fellow countryman and former Feyenoord team-mate Regi Blinker, plus the less exotic Darren Jackson, and seems assured of a bright future.

BEST SEASON 1

A hundred years ago, Celtic went through an entire League season without losing a game. It's true that in those days the Scottish First Division comprised only ten teams and so each played only 18 fixtures, but it is still a remarkable achievement.

Celtic had finished the 1896-97 campaign in fourth position, Hearts having won the Championship, and supporters can hardly have been expecting great things from 1897-98. However, the Celts beat Hibs 4-1 in the opening fixture, drew at the home of their Edinburgh rivals 0-0, and then won the next three games (the final one being a 4-0 away win at Rangers) to place themselves firmly at the top of the table.

Even though Celtic were almost invincible, they normally scored no more than two or three goals – although they did put six and nine past Clyde and another six past Partick Thistle. The defence conceded an exact average of a goal per game but, at a time when goalkeepers received little protection from referees, Celtic's custodian had a hard time of it. Dan McArthur, the 'unbeatable little demon', was arguably the best keeper ever to play at Parkhead. He was often injured, but missed only one game in 1897-98.

At the heart of the defence was Davie Russell, a centre-half with a stunning long-distance shot, who played in every game and scored a total of nine goals, while Jim Welford – who played cricket for both Durham and Warwickshire – was at right-back for most of the season.

The chief goalscorer was centre-forward Dod Allan. He had been with Liverpool, and was to return to Merseyside after just the one season with Celtic. His style of play didn't really fit in with Celtic's patient build-up (perhaps Liverpool really invented the long-ball game!) but he still managed to score 15 goals in 16 League outings, netting five times in the 9-1 victory at Clyde. Sadly, Allan was to die from tuberculosis 18 months after returning to Liverpool.

Celtic's remaining scorers in 1897-98 were Jack Reynolds (1), Pat Gilhooly (5), John Campbell, who had two spells with Celtic and in all scored 109 goals in 215 appearances (7), Alex King, who used to take over in goal whenever McArthur was knocked unconscious (3), Adam Henderson (4) and Peter Somers, who was just beginning his Celtic career (3).

With 15 games won and 3 drawn, it was quite a season…

1897-98 LEAGUE RECORD		
Opponents	**Home**	**Away**
Clyde	6-1	9-1
Dundee	2-1	2-1
Hearts	3-2	0-0
Hibernian	4-1	2-1
Partick Thistle	3-1	6-3
Rangers	0-0	4-0
St Bernard's	5-1	2-0
St Mirren	3-0	0-0
Third Lanark	4-0	1-0

DERBY  FOCUS

There are derbies, and there's the Glasgow derby. For all sorts of reasons – many, it must be said, nothing to do with football – the clash of the Glasgow giants has always been the prime fixture in Scottish, and indeed many would say British, footballing calendar.

Celtic versus Rangers, the clash of the Glasgow giants, has always been the prime fixture in the Scottish footballing calendar, ranking up there with Liverpool and Manchester in the local derby stakes. It may happen at least four times a season these days, but passions remain undimmed both on and off the park.

• • • • • ⚽ • • • • •

The Old Firm rivalry began with the formation of Celtic Football and Athletic Club in 1888. Rangers, for their part, had been established some 16 years previously, and the teams locked horns in Celtic's very first match. The odds favoured the established team, but it was the Bhoys in green that ran out 5-2 winners in front of a 2,000-strong crowd paying sixpence a head. Yet the most fascinating fact must surely be that the two sets of players chose to wind down together by sharing tea (and, apparently, indulging in a spot of community singing) in a local hall. Hardly the image of the fixture in more recent years...

The Scottish League opened for business in 1890-91, and as you'd expect both Celtic and Rangers were founder members. September 1898's League meeting at Parkhead attracted a crowd of 44,868, underlining the fact that the rivalry was already highly profitable in terms of bodies through the turnstiles.

The first Old Firm clash in the Scottish Cup had taken place in 1890, a Willie Groves goal being enough to take the honours. Next came a Semi-Final meeting in 1892 when Celtic raced into a 4-0 half-time lead before letting it slip somewhat and ending 5-3 winners. The clubs first met in the Final two years later, Rangers proving the winners by three goals to one. The sides would clash again in 1899, Celtic this time taking delight in depriving their rivals of a League and Cup Double thanks to goals by Johnny Hodge and Sandy McMahon. The winning margin was doubled the following season, after a 2-2 Semi-Final draw. (There had also, meanwhile, been meetings in the Glasgow Cup and Glasgow Charity Cups, which brought some hair-raising results.)

The first decade of the new century undeniably belonged to Celtic, who snapped up six successive Championships between 1904 and 1910. There could have been a hat-trick of 'Doubles' had it not been for the match of 1909 when the Scottish FA withheld the Cup due to a pitch invasion. Crowds peaked at the end of the inter-war period when the Ne'erday (New Year's Day) games of 1938 and 1939 drew crowds of 85,000 and 118,567, the latter still a record attendance for a League game in Britain. Though the crowds of today don't measure up to those of yesteryear for safety reasons, passions remain high, and even today Old Firm reserve games sometimes attract five-figure gates.

Derby games are supposed to be hard-fought, close-run affairs, but the League Cup Final of October 1957, which Celtic won with embarrassing ease by 7-1, was the exception that proved the rule. This was to prove a false dawn, however. From then until 1965, Celtic would fail to pick up any of Scotland's three major trophies, while their rivals ran rampant. Jock Stein changed all that – and his return was to herald a golden age.

After an up-and-down 1970s, the 1980s was the decade when a century of history was turned on its head. The Glasgow giants had been caught by a 'New Firm' of Aberdeen and Dundee United which had emerged to challenge the big city's dominance. Rangers responded by employing Graeme Souness and giving him an open cheque book – and, in the face of this Ibrox revival that followed, the Celtic board went through managers as if discarding playing cards.

Former players Billy McNeill (twice), David Hay and Lou Macari all tried and failed to stimulate a lasting Parkhead revival, while Eire international Liam Brady found Glasgow was hardly the place to learn the managerial ropes. Only with the return of another ex-player, Tommy Burns, in 1994 would fortunes pick up and a true challenge be mounted.

On paper, the 1995-96 season saw Rangers complete their third Double of the 1990s. Yet Celtic's amazing undefeated League run, which began back in October and extended to the end of the season, gave their fans cause to cheer and their neighbours something to think about. With the arrival of Dutch coach Wim Jansen in 1997 and his initial Coca-Cola Cup success late that same year, Parkhead was becoming even more cosmopolitan than Ibrox, players like Blinker, Larsen and Brattbakk savouring their first taste of Glasgow football.

With the 1998 Ne'erday clash ending a decisive 2-0 in Celtic's favour, little wonder the feeling was that the pendulum was swinging back towards the green side of Glasgow.

The story so far

	P	W	D	L	F	A
League	244	74	73	97	318	359
FA Cup	40	19	8	13	62	52
League Cup	41	19	2	20	61	58
War Games etc	166	51	36	79	244	299
Total	**491**	**163**	**119**	**209**	**685**	**768**

CELTIC'S TOP 10 DERBY APPEARANCES			
1	Paul McStay	1981-97	66
2=	Roy Aitken	1974-90	58
2=	Packy Bonner	1978-95	58
2=	Billy McNeill	1957-75	58
5	Danny McGrain	1967-87	53
6	Peter Grant	1982-97	47
7	Tommy Burns	1973-89	45
8=	Jimmy Johnstone	1961-75	44
8=	Bobby Lennox	1961-78, 1978-80	44
10	Bobby Evans	1944-60	43

THROUGH THE YEARS
MARCH

1891
March
21

This month saw Celtic's first ever Scottish League game with Rangers. The Celts had made a good start to their first League season but this was to be the beginning of a rivalry which was to last for a century and beyond. The result, which most neutral observers (if there were any!) thought fair, was a 2-2 draw – the Celtic goals coming from Peter Dowds and Johnny Campbell. This was, however, the first League game at Parkhead which Celtic had not won.

1923
March
31

On the last day of the month, Celtic won the Scottish Cup for the tenth time, beating Hibernian with a headed goal from Joe Cassidy – a forward who scored 104 times during his Celtic career. It was not the first time the Final had been played during March, but it was the first time the Celts had carried off the trophy during that particular month.

1954

March

Celtic won the Scottish League Championship at the end of season 1953–54, having been victorious in their last nine matches. During March they scored 17 goals in four games, beating East Fife and Stirling Albion at home 4–1 and 4–0 respectively, and beating Airdrie and Partick Thistle away 6–0 and 3–1.

1968
March
16

Bobby Lennox had been sent off in the World Championship play-off in Montevideo in November 1967. It took a very long time, but in March 1968 he was exonerated by the Scottish Football Association. It had been a case of mistaken identity.

1994
March
4

With Celtic Football Club in severe financial trouble, Fergus McCann attempted to buy control. He was at first rebuffed, but on 4 March his wish was granted. Most fans were delighted.

FA CUP RECORD

Celtic's Cup career took four seasons to
bear fruit — but that first win has been
followed by many more. Here is the
complete statistical story.

Stage	Opponents	Score
1888-89		
Round 1	Shettleston	5-1
Round 2	Cowlairs	8-0
Round 3	Albion Rovers	4-1
Round 4	St Bernard's	4-1
Round 5	Clyde	9-2
Quarter-Final	East Stirling	2-1
Semi-Final	Dumbarton	4-1
Final	Third Lanark	1-2
1889-90		
Round 1	Queen's Park	*0-0, 1-2
	* *Match abandoned*	
1890-91		
Round 1	Rangers	1-0
Round 2	Carfin Shamrock	2-2, 3-1
Round 3	Wishaw Thistle	6-2
Round 4	Our Boys	3-1
Round 5	Royal Albert	2-0
Quarter-Final	Dumbarton	0-3
1891-92		
Round 5	St Mirren	4-2
Round 6	Kilmarnock	3-0
Quarter-Final	Cowlairs	4-1
Semi-Final	Rangers	5-3
Final	Queen's Park	5-1

Stage	Opponents	Score
	1892-93	
Round 1	Linthouse	3-1
Round 2	Fifth Kirkcudbright RV	7-0
Quarter-Final	Third Lanark	5-1
Semi-Final	St Bernard's	5-0
Final	Queen's Park	1-2
	1893-94	
Round 1	Hurlford	6-0
Round 2	Albion Rovers	7-0
Quarter-Final	St Bernard's	8-1
Semi-Final	Third Lanark	5-3
Final	Rangers	1-3
	1894-95	
Round 1	Queen's Park	4-1
Round 2	Hibernian	*0-2, 2-0
*Match replayed after a protest		
Quarter-Final	Dundee	0-1
	1895-96	
Round 1	Queen's Park	2-4
	1896-97	
Round 1	Arthurlie	2-4
	1897-98	
Round 1	Arthurlie	7-0
Round 2	Third Lanark	2-3
	1898-99	
Round 1	Sixth Galloway RV	8-1
Round 2	St Bernard's	3-0
Quarter-Final	Queen's Park	2-1
Semi-Final	Port Glasgow	4-2
Final	Rangers	2-0

Stage	Opponents	Score
1899-1900		
Round 1	Bo'ness	7-1
Round 2	Port Glasgow	5-1
Quarter-Final	Kilmarnock	4-0
Semi-Final	Rangers	2-2, 4-0
Final	Queen's Park	4-3
1900-01		
Round 1	Rangers	1-0
Round 2	Kilmarnock	6-0
Quarter-Final	Dundee	1-0
Semi-Final	St Mirren	1-0
Final	Hearts	3-4
1901-02		
Round 1	Thornliebank	3-0
Round 2	Arbroath	3-2
Quarter-Final	Hearts	1-1, 2-1
Semi-Final	St Mirren	3-2
Final	Hibernian	0-1
1902-03		
Round 1	St Mirren	0-0, 1-1, 4-0
Round 2	Port Glasgow	2-0
Quarter-Final	Rangers	0-3
1903-04		
Round 1	Stanley	Walkover
Round 2	St Bernard's	4-0
Quarter-Final	Dundee	1-1, 0-0, 5-0
Semi-Final	Third Lanark	2-1
Final	Rangers	3-2
1904-05		
Round 1	Dumfries	2-1
Round 2	Lochgelly United	3-0
Quarter-Final	Partick Thistle	3-0
Semi-Final	Rangers	0-2

Stage	Opponents	Score
1905-06		
Round 1	Dundee	2-1
Round 2	Bo'ness	3-0
Quarter-Final	Hearts	1-2
1906-07		
Round 1	Clyde	2-1
Round 2	Morton	0-0, 1-1, 2-1
Quarter-Final	Rangers	3-0
Semi-Final	Hibernian	0-0, 0-0, 3-0
Final	Hearts	3-0
1907-08		
Round 1	Peebles Rovers	4-0
Round 2	Rangers	2-1
Quarter-Final	Raith Rovers	3-0
Semi-Final	Aberdeen	1-0
Final	St Mirren	5-1
1908-09		
Round 1	Leith Athletic	4-2
Round 2	Port Glasgow	4-0
Quarter-Final	Airdrieonians	3-1
Semi-Final	Clyde	0-0, 2-0
Final	Rangers	2-2, 1-1

Following a riot at the replay, the competition was abandoned

Stage	Opponents	Score
1909-10		
Round 1	Dumbarton	2-1
Round 2	Third Lanark	3-1
Quarter-Final	Aberdeen	2-1
Semi-Final	Clyde	1-3

Stage	Opponents	Score
1910-11		
Round 1	St Mirren	2-0
Round 2	Galston	1-0
Quarter-Final	Clyde	1-0
Semi-Final	Aberdeen	1-0
Final	Hamilton A	0-0, 2-0
1911-12		
Round 1	Dunfermline	1-0
Round 2	East Stirling	3-0
Quarter-Final	Aberdeen	2-2, 2-0
Semi-Final	Hearts	3-0
Final	Clyde	2-0
1912-13		
Round 2	Arbroath	4-0
Round 3	Peebles Rovers	3-0
Quarter-Final	Hearts	0-1
1913-14		
Round 2	Clyde	0-0, 2-0
Round 3	Forfar Athletic	5-0
Quarter-Final	Motherwell	3-1
Semi-Final	Third Lanark	2-0
Final	Hibernian	0-0, 4-1
1919-20		
Round 2	Dundee	3-1
Round 3	Partick Thistle	2-0
Quarter-Final	Rangers	0-1
1920-21		
Round 2	Vale of Leven	3-0
Round 3	East Fife	3-1
Quarter-Final	Hearts	1-2

Stage	Opponents	Score
1921-22		
Round 1	Montrose	4-0
Round 2	Third Lanark	1-0
Round 3	Hamilton A	1-3
1922-23		
Round 1	Lochgelly United	3-2
Round 2	Hurlford	4-0
Round 3	East Fife	2-1
Quarter-Final	Raith Rovers	1-0
Semi-Final	Motherwell	2-0
Final	Hibernian	1-0
1923-24		
Round 1	Kilmarnock	0-2
1924-25		
Round 1	Third Lanark	5-1
Round 2	Alloa	2-1
Round 3	Solway Star	2-0
Quarter-Final	St Mirren	0-0, 1-1, 1-0
Semi-Final	Rangers	5-0
Final	Dundee	2-1
1925-26		
Round 1	Kilmarnock	5-0
Round 2	Hamilton A	4-0
Round 3	Hearts	4-0
Quarter-Final	Dumbarton	6-1
Semi-Final	Aberdeen	2-1
Final	St Mirren	0-2

Stage	Opponents	Score
1926-27		
Round 1	Queen of the South	0-0, 4-1
Round 2	Brechin City	6-3
Round 3	Dundee	4-2
Quarter-Final	Bo'ness	5-2
Semi-Final	Falkirk	1-0
Final	East Fife	3-1
1927-28		
Round 1	Bathgate	3-1
Round 2	Keith	6-1
Round 3	Alloa	2-0
Quarter-Final	Motherwell	2-0
Semi-Final	Queen's Park	2-1
Final	Rangers	0-4
1928-29		
Round 1	Arthurlie	5-1
Round 2	East Stirling	3-0
Round 3	Arbroath	4-1
Quarter-Final	Motherwell	0-0, 2-1
Semi-Final	Kilmarnock	0-1
1929-30		
Round 1	Inverness Caledonian	6-0
Round 2	Arbroath	5-0
Round 3	St Mirren	1-3
1930-31		
Round 1	East Fife	2-1
Round 2	Dundee United	3-2
Round 3	Morton	4-1
Quarter-Final	Aberdeen	4-0
Semi-Final	Kilmarnock	3-0
Final	Motherwell	2-2, 4-2

Stage	Opponents	Score
	1931-32	
Round 1	Falkirk	3-2
Round 2	St Johnstone	4-2
Round 3	Motherwell	0-2
	1932-33	
Round 1	Dunfermline	7-1
Round 2	Falkirk	2-0
Round 3	Partick Thistle	2-1
Quarter-Final	Albion Rovers	1-1, 3-1
Semi-Final	Hearts	0-0, 2-1
Final	Motherwell	1-0
	1933-34	
Round 1	Dalbeattie Star	6-0
Round 2	Ayr United	3-2
Round 3	Falkirk	3-1
Quarter-Final	St Mirren	0-2
	1934-35	
Round 1	Montrose	4-1
Round 2	Partick Thistle	1-1, 3-1
Round 3	Bye	
Quarter-Final	Aberdeen	1-3
	1935-36	
Round 1	Berwick	Walkover
Round 2	St Johnstone	1-2
	1936-37	
Round 1	Stenhousemuir	1-1, 2-0
Round 2	Albion Rovers	5-2
Round 3	East Fife	3-0
Quarter-Final	Motherwell	4-4, 2-1
Semi-Final	Clyde	2-0
Final	Aberdeen	2-1

Stage	Opponents	Score
	1937-38	
Round 1	Third Lanark	2-1
Round 2	Nithsdale Wanderers	5-0
Round 3	Kilmarnock	1-2
	1938-39	
Round 1	Burntisland Shipyard	8-3
Round 2	Montrose	7-1
Round 3	Hearts	2-2, 2-1
Quarter-Final	Motherwell	1-3
	1946-47	
Round 1	Dundee	1-2
	1947-48	
Round 2	Cowdenbeath	3-0
Round 3	Motherwell	1-0
Quarter-Final	Montrose	4-0
Semi-Final	Morton	0-1
	1948-49	
Round 1	Dundee United	3-4
	1949-50	
Round 1	Brechin City	3-0
Round 2	Third Lanark	1-1, 4-1
Round 3	Aberdeen	0-1
	1950-51	
Round 1	East Fife	2-2, 4-2
Round 2	Duns	4-0
Round 3	Hearts	2-1
Quarter-Final	Aberdeen	3-0
Semi-Final	Raith Rovers	3-2
Final	Motherwell	1-0

Stage	Opponents	Score
	1951-52	
Round 1	Third Lanark	0-0, 1-2
	1952-53	
Round 1	Eyemouth	4-0
Round 2	Stirling Albion	1-1, 3-0
Round 3	Falkirk	3-2
Quarter-Final	Rangers	0-2
	1953-54	
Round 2	Falkirk	2-1
Round 3	Stirling Albion	4-3
Quarter-Final	Hamilton A	2-1
Semi-Final	Motherwell	2-2, 3-1
Final	Aberdeen	2-1
	1954-55	
Round 5	Alloa	4-2
Round 6	Kilmarnock	1-1, 1-0
Quarter-Final	Hamilton A	2-1
Semi-Final	Airdrieonians	2-2, 2-0
Final	Clyde	1-1, 0-1
	1955-56	
Round 5	Morton	2-0
Round 6	Ayr United	3-0
Quarter-Final	Airdrieonians	2-1
Semi-Final	Clyde	2-1
Final	Hearts	1-3
	1956-57	
Round 5	Forres Mechanics	5-0
Round 6	Rangers	4-4, 2-0
Quarter-Final	St Mirren	2-1
Semi-Final	Kilmarnock	1-1, 1-3

Stage	Opponents	Score
	1957-58	
Round 1	Airdrieonians	4-3
Round 2	Stirling Albion	7-2
Round 3	Clyde	0-2
	1958-59	
Round 1	Albion Rovers	4-0
Round 2	Clyde	1-1, 4-3
Round 3	Rangers	2-1
Quarter-Final	Stirling Albion	3-1
Semi-Final	St Mirren	0-4
	1959-60	
Round 2	St Mirren	1-1, 4-4, 5-2
Round 3	Elgin City	2-1
Quarter-Final	Partick Thistle	2-0
Semi-Final	Rangers	1-1, 1-4
	1960-61	
Round 1	Falkirk	3-1
Round 2	Montrose	6-0
Round 3	Raith Rovers	4-1
Quarter-Final	Hibernian	1-1, 1-0
Semi-Final	Airdrieonians	4-0
Final	Dunfermline Athletic	0-0, 0-2
	1961-62	
Round 1	Cowdenbeath	5-1
Round 2	Morton	3-1
Round 3	Hearts	4-3
Quarter-Final	Third Lanark	4-4, 4-0
Semi-Final	St Mirren	1-3

Stage	Opponents	Score
1962-63		
Round 1	Falkirk	2-0
Round 2	Hearts	3-1
Round 3	Gala Fairydean	6-0
Quarter-Final	St Mirren	1-0
Semi-Final	Raith Rovers	5-2
Final	Rangers	1-1, 0-3
1963-64		
Round 1	Eyemouth	3-0
Round 2	Morton	3-1
Round 3	Airdrieonians	4-1
Quarter-Final	Rangers	0-2
1964-65		
Round 1	St Mirren	3-0
Round 2	Queen's Park	1-0
Quarter-Final	Kilmarnock	3-2
Semi-Final	Motherwell	2-2, 3-0
Final	Dunfermline Athletic	3-2
1965-66		
Round 1	Stranraer	4-0
Round 2	Dundee	2-0
Quarter-Final	Hearts	3-3, 3-1
Semi-Final	Dunfermline Athletic	2-0
Final	Rangers	0-0, 0-1
1966-67		
Round 1	Arbroath	4-0
Round 2	Elgin City	7-0
Quarter-Final	Queen's Park	5-3
Semi-Final	Clyde	0-0, 2-0
Final	Aberdeen	2-0
1967-68		
Round 1	Dunfermline Athletic	0-2

Stage	Opponents	Score
	1968-69	
Round 1	Partick Thistle	3-3, 8-1
Round 2	Clyde	0-0, 3-0
Quarter-Final	St Johnstone	3-2
Semi-Final	Morton	4-1
Final	Rangers	4-0
	1969-70	
Round 1	Dunfermline Athletic	2-1
Round 2	Dundee United	4-0
Quarter-Final	Rangers	3-1
Semi-Final	Dundee	2-1
Final	Aberdeen	1-3
	1970-71	
Round 3	Queen of the South	5-1
Round 4	Dunfermline Athletic	1-1, 1-0
Quarter-Final	Raith Rovers	7-1
Semi-Final	Airdrieonians	3-3, 2-0
Final	Rangers	1-1, 2-1
	1971-72	
Round 3	Albion Rovers	5-0
Round 4	Dundee	4-0
Quarter-Final	Hearts	1-1, 1-0
Semi-Final	Kilmarnock	3-1
Final	Hibernian	6-1
	1972-73	
Round 3	East Fife	4-1
Round 4	Motherwell	4-0
Quarter-Final	Aberdeen	0-0, 1-0
Semi-Final	Dundee	0-0, 3-0
Final	Rangers	2-3

Stage	Opponents	Score
1973-74		
Round 3	Clydebank	6-1
Round 4	Stirling Albion	6-1
Quarter-Final	Motherwell	2-2, 1-0
Semi-Final	Dundee	1-0
Final	Dundee United	3-0
1974-75		
Round 3	Hibernian	2-0
Round 4	Clydebank	4-1
Quarter-Final	Dumbarton	2-1
Semi-Final	Dundee	1-0
Final	Airdrieonians	3-1
1975-76		
Round 3	Motherwell	2-3
1976-77		
Round 3	Airdrieonians	1-1, 5-0
Round 4	Ayr United	1-1, 3-1
Quarter-Final	Queen of the South	5-1
Semi-Final	Dundee	2-0
Final	Rangers	1-0
1977-78		
Round 3	Dundee	7-1
Round 4	Kilmarnock	1-1, 0-1
1978-79		
Round 3	Montrose	4-2
Round 4	Berwick Rangers	3-0
Quarter-Final	Aberdeen	1-1, 1-2

Stage	Opponents	Score
1979-80		
Round 3	Raith Rovers	2-1
Round 4	St Mirren	1-1, 3-2
Quarter-Final	Morton	2-0
Semi-Final	Hibernian	5-0
Final	Rangers	1-0
1980-81		
Round 3	Berwick Rangers	2-0
Round 4	Stirling Albion	3-0
Quarter-Final	East Stirling	2-0
Semi-Final	Dundee United	0-0, 2-3
1981-82		
Round 3	Queen of the South	4-0
Round 4	Aberdeen	0-1
1982-83		
Round 3	Clydebank	3-0
Round 4	Dunfermline Athletic	3-0
Quarter-Final	Hearts	4-1
Semi-Final	Aberdeen	0-1
1983-84		
Round 3	Berwick Rangers	4-0
Round 4	East Fife	6-0
Quarter-Final	Motherwell	6-0
Semi-Final	St Mirren	2-1
Final	Aberdeen	1-2
1984-85		
Round 3	Hamilton A	2-1
Round 4	Inverness Athletic	6-0
Quarter-Final	Dundee	1-1, 2-1
Semi-Final	Motherwell	0-0, 3-0
Final	Dundee United	2-1

Stage	Opponents	Score
	1985-86	
Round 3	St Johnstone	2-0
Round 4	Queen's Park	2-1
Quarter-Final	Hibernian	3-4
	1986-87	
Round 3	Aberdeen	2-2, 0-0, 1-0
Round 4	Hearts	0-1
	1987-88	
Round 3	Stranraer	1-0
Round 4	Hibernian	0-0, 1-0
Quarter-Final	Partick Thistle	3-0
Semi-Final	Hearts	2-1
Final	Dundee United	2-1
	1988-89	
Round 3	Dumbarton	2-0
Round 4	Clydebank	4-1
Quarter-Final	Hearts	2-1
Semi-Final	Hibernian	3-1
Final	Rangers	1-0
	1989-90	
Round 3	Forfar Athletic	2-1
Round 4	Rangers	1-0
Quarter-Final	Dunfermline Athletic	0-0, 3-0
Semi-Final	Clydebank	2-0
Final	Aberdeen	0-0
	Celtic lost 8-9 on penalties	
	1990-91	
Round 3	Forfar Athletic	2-0
Round 4	St Mirren	3-0
Quarter-Final	Rangers	2-0
Semi-Final	Motherwell	0-0, 2-4

Stage	Opponents	Score
1991-92		
Round 3	Montrose	6-0
Round 4	Dundee United	2-1
Quarter-Final	Morton	3-0
Semi-Final	Rangers	0-1
1992-93		
Round 3	Clyde	0-0, 1-0
Round 4	Falkirk	0-2
1993-94		
Round 3	Motherwell	0-1
1994-95		
Round 3	St Mirren	2-0
Round 4	Meadowbank Thistle	3-0
Quarter-Final	Kilmarnock	1-0
Semi-Final	Hibernian	0-0, 3-1
Final	Airdrieonians	1-0
1995-96		
Round 3	Whitehill Welfare	3-0
Round 4	Raith Rovers	2-0
Quarter-Final	Dundee United	2-1
Semi-Final	Rangers	1-2
1996-97		
Round 3	Clydebank	5-0
Round 4	Hibernian	1-1, 2-0
Quarter-Final	Rangers	2-0
Semi-Final	Falkirk	1-1, 0-1

FA Cup Record Club By Club

Opposition	P	W	D	L	F-A
Aberdeen	25	12	6	7	32-22
Airdrieonians	13	10	3	—	36-13
Albion Rovers	7	6	1	—	29-5
Alloa	3	3	—	—	8-3
Arbroath	4	4	—	—	16-2
Arthurlie	2	1	—	1	9-4
Ayr United	4	3	1	—	10-4
Bathgate	1	1	—	—	3-1
Berwick Rangers	3	3	—	—	9-0
Bo'ness	3	3	—	—	15-3
Brechin City	2	2	—	—	9-3
Burntisland S	1	1	—	—	8-3
Carfin Shamrock	2	1	1	—	5-3
Clyde	22	12	7	3	35-16
Clydebank	6	6	—	—	24-3
Cowdenbeath	2	2	—	—	8-1
Cowlairs	2	2	—	—	12-1
Dalbeattie Star	1	1	—	—	6-0
Dumbarton	6	5	—	1	16-7
Dumfries	1	1	—	—	2-1
Dundee	20	14	4	2	42-12
Dundee United	10	7	1	2	23-13
Dunfermline	12	7	3	2	16-8
Duns	1	1	—	—	4-0
East Fife	9	8	1	—	29-9
East Stirling	3	3	—	—	7-1
Elgin City	2	2	—	—	9-1
Eyemouth	2	2	—	—	7-0
Falkirk	10	8	—	2	18-10
5th KRV	1	1	—	—	7-0
Forfar Athletic	3	3	—	—	9-1
Forres Mechanics	1	1	—	—	5-0
Gala Fairydean	1	1	—	—	6-0
Galston	1	1	—	—	1-0
Hamilton A	7	5	1	1	13-6
Hearts	25	14	5	6	50-32
Hibernian	22	13	6	3	38-13
Hurlford	2	2	—	—	10-0
Inverness Athletic	1	1	—	—	6-0
Inverness Cal	1	1	—	—	6-0
Keith	1	1	—	—	6-1
Kilmarnock	17	9	3	5	34-15
Leith Athletic	1	1	—	—	4-2
Linthouse	1	1	—	—	3-1
Lochgelly United	1	1	—	—	3-2
Meadowbank Th	1	1	—	—	3-0
Montrose	7	7	—	—	35-4
Morton	11	8	2	1	24-7
Motherwell	26	14	8	4	53-30
Nithsdale W	1	1	—	—	5-0
Our Boys	1	1	—	—	3-1
Partick Thistle	8	6	2	—	24-7
Peebles Rovers	2	2	—	—	7-0
Port Glasgow	4	4	—	—	13-2
Queen of South	5	4	1	—	18-3
Queen's Park	10	7	—	3	27-18
Raith Rovers	8	8	—	—	28-7
Rangers	39	20	8	11	64-46
Royal Albert	1	1	—	—	2-0
Shettleston	1	1	—	—	5-1
6th Galloway RV	1	1	—	—	8-1
Solway Star	1	1	—	—	2-0
St Bernard's	5	5	—	—	24-2
St Johnstone	3	2	—	1	6-4
St Mirren	27	15	7	5	51-33
Stenhousemuir	2	1	1	—	3-1
Stirling Albion	7	6	1	—	27-8
Stranraer	2	2	—	—	5-0
Third Lanark	16	10	3	3	42-21
Thornliebank	1	1	—	—	3-0
Vale of Leven	1	1	—	—	3-0
Whitehill Welfare	1	1	—	—	3-0
Wishaw Thistle	1	1	—	—	6-2

CREAM OF THE CONTINENT

For obvious reasons, Celtic has always had a number of Irish footballers on its books, but early on most players inevitably came from the Glasgow area.

There were other Scots of course and even one or two real foreigners – from England! In 1913 one Ebenezer Owers (known as Ginger) born in West Ham, London, arrived at Parkhead on loan from Clyde and made 16 appearances for Celtic before returning to Shawfield.

Before the advent of Ebenezer, the Celts had a Welshman on their books. Leigh Richmond Roose was a famous amateur goalkeeper, a Doctor of Bacteriology, and a bit of a character. Born near Wrexham, he played just one game while on loan from Sunderland during an injury crisis. Known for practical jokes, he would arrive with his hands bandaged, and then announce that he was quite fit to play.

Celtic's first genuine foreign player of note was probably another goalkeeper – Joe Kennaway. Born in Montreal, Kennaway came across to take over the gloves following the sad demise of John Thomson in 1931. Another keeper, Rolando Ugolini, entered the service of Celtic in 1944 – although he only just qualifies as foreign, having been born in Lucca, Italy, and brought to Scotland as a three-year-old. Konrad Kapler, on the other hand, had been in the Polish Army and was signed from Forres Mechanics in 1947. An outside-left, he played eight times for Celtic and was allowed to go free in 1949. He died in Rochdale in 1991.

Mass signings of foreign players have been a recent phenomenon, but Jock Stein spotted an Icelandic possibility in June 1975. With Stein badly injured in a car crash a month later, it was left for Sean Fallon to sign utility player Johannes Edvaldsson. Tulsa Roughnecks claimed Edvaldsson in February 1980, but not before he had made 188 appearances in the jersey and scored 36 goals. He was also capped 16 times for his native land while a Celtic player, and gained the affectionate nickname of 'Shuggie'.

In 1989 Celtic decided to give matchday magazine typesetters a double nightmare by signing a pair of Polish players – Dariusz 'Jacki' Dziekanowski and Dariusz Wdowczyk. The first Dariusz played 66 times and scored 22 goals before departing for Bristol City, while the second made 148 appearances before being released in May 1994.

Rudi Vata signed for Celtic in August 1994 and became an instant hit with the Parkhead faithful. The following year saw Pierre van Hooijdonk follow his example. One of the tallest men ever to play for Celtic at six foot five inches, he came with a proven goalscoring record and again became an instant hit – especially when he scored the only goal of the 1995 Scottish Cup Final. He left for Nottingham Forest towards the end of the 1996–97 season after a disagreement over money: many were sad to see him go.

Another foreign hotshot to make an impression was Andreas Thom, who, having moved from East to West Germany before unification, made his Celtic debut on 5 August 1995 in the match to celebrate the opening of the new North Stand. He scored on his debut in a Coca-Cola Cup game at Ayr, but returned to Germany in 1998.

The current side, the first to be managed by a man from outside the British Isles, has no shortage of exotic names: Henrik Larsson, Harald Brattbakk and Regi Blinker among them. It seems that no stone will be left unturned in Wim Jansen's efforts to restore Celtic to their rightful place.

THROUGH THE YEARS
APRIL

1889
April
13

Less than 12 months after Celtic had played their first game, two of their players, James Kelly and James McLaren, were selected to play for Scotland against England at the Oval in London. McLaren scored with the last kick of the match to secure a 3–2 victory for the visiting side.

1892
April
9

Celtic won the Scottish Cup for the first time. In the Final, replayed at Ibrox because conditions for the first game had been deemed too bad, they beat Queen's Park 5–1, the goals coming from Sandy McMahon (2), Johnny Campbell (2) and an own goal by Sellar.

1909
April
10

Celtic reached the Scottish Cup Final, and played Rangers at Hampden. The result was a 2–2 draw, so the match was replayed a week later. In the second encounter, Jimmy Quinn scored an equaliser (as he had done in the first game) and this time the match was drawn 1-1. Fans of both sides expected extra time to be played, and when this did not happen a riot of unprecedented ferocity ensued. The SFA eventually decided to withhold the trophy.

1916
April
15

Having beaten Raith Rovers 6-0 at Parkhead in an afternoon game, Celtic then travelled to Motherwell for an evening game, which they won 3-1. Patsy Gallagher scored a hat-trick in the first game but he failed to score in the evening...

1937
April
24

The Scottish Cup Final against Aberdeen attracted a record crowd of 146,433. This is the highest official attendance figure for any game between two European clubs. Celtic won 2-1, with goals from Willie Buchan and Johnny Crum.

1970
April

Celtic met Leeds United in the Semi-Final of the European Cup. They won 1-0 at Elland Road and then beat United 2-1 at Parkhead before losing to Feyenoord in May.

20 THINGS YOU PROBABLY NEVER KNEW...

1 A few months after the club was formed, Celtic reached the final of the Scottish Cup. They were to play Third Lanark, but on the day it was snowing hard. The Scottish Football Association ruled that the game should be played, as a large crowd had already gathered. Both teams protested, but were given to understand that the game would be classed as a friendly, so went ahead believing that the actual Final would be played on another day.

Third Lanark won 3-0 – and then, to the amazement of Celtic, they claimed the Cup! Celtic were incensed and the SFA eventually ordered a replay...which Celtic lost 2-1.

2 Alec Bennett (1903-08) won 18 Scottish caps, while rugby prop forward Sandy Carmichael, who was his grandson, would later tour with the British Lions and play 50 times for Scotland.

3 Alec Boden (1943-56) became a scout for Celtic when his playing days were over. On one occasion he was dispatched to look at a young Glasgow United player called Vic Davidson. Young Vic did quite well, but Alec's eye was caught by one of his team mates, a certain Kenneth Dalglish. Alec suggested that Celtic should monitor the progress of this likely-looking lad...and the rest is history.

4 When Celtic beat Inter Milan to win the European Cup in 1967, four players, all of whom played in one or more of the earlier rounds, missed out. They were: Willie O'Neill, John Hughes, Joe McBride and Charlie Gallagher.

5 Billy McNeil won seven Scottish Cup winner's medals – in 1965, 1967, 1969, 1971, 1972, 1974 and 1975. Jimmy McMenemy also won seven, but one of these was gained while he was with Partick Thistle.

6 Charlie Tully's 1955 Scottish Cup Final runners-up medal was sold at auction in 1971 for just £19. The buyer was Celtic Football Club.

7 Andy McAtee's Championship medal came up for auction in Glasgow six years later. This time, Celtic were outbid by a supporter, who paid £60 for it.

8 The Scotland team which beat Northern Ireland 2-1 at Hampden Park in November 1967 contained six Celtic players – Tommy Gemmell, Bobby Murdoch, John Clark, Steve Chalmers, Joe McBride and Bobby Lennox. Of these, only Joe McBride had been absent from Celtic's European Cup-winning side a few months earlier.

9 Bolton Wanderers wanted £2.2 million for Andy Walker in 1994. Celtic offered £220,000 and a tribunal set the figure at £550,000. Transfer fees are very strange things…

10 Supporters of south-west London club Fulham have been known to chant: 'There's only one Micky Conroy'. But

Celtic had *two* Michael Conroys – Mike Conroy senior (1953-60) and Mike Conroy junior (1978-82).

11 Goalkeeper Joe Cullen (1892-97) lost the ball a few times in his career, and he also lost his 1894 Scottish Cup Final runners-up medal. It was found in the street in Brisbane, Australia, some 30 years later and returned to Willie Maley at Celtic. Mr Maley kept it on his desk until it was stolen during a burglary, but was later posted back to him. This time, the Celtic manager managed to hold on to it.

12 In 1994-95 Celtic played all their home games at Hampden Park while their own ground was being re-built. The change of venue did not help their League performances and they finished the season in fourth place, a full 18 points adrift of Rangers. They did however reach the Scottish Cup Final, conceding only one goal along the way, and they carried off the trophy when Pierre Van Hooijdonk scored the only goal of the game against First Division Airdrieonians.

13 Hotshot full-back Tommy Gemmell took 34 penalties for Celtic, scoring from them on 31 occasions.

14 The legendary Jimmy McGrory was Europe's top scorer in 1926-27, with 49 goals. In 1935-36 he went one better.

15 In September 1963, Celtic were 4-0 up at home to Third Lanark after just 16 minutes. By half-time the score was 4-3, and early in the second period Third Lanark scored an equaliser. No more goals were scored in that amazing game.

16 In January 1965 Celtic beat Aberdeen 8-0. John Hughes scored five of the goals – wearing Billy McNeill's training shoes on the hard ground.

17 Rangers and Celtic were each fined £20,000 when fans invaded the pitch following the Scottish Cup final in 1980, which Celtic won 1-0 in extra time.

18 In the last game of his first period with Celtic, in May 1983, Charlie Nicholas scored twice from the spot as the Bhoys beat Rangers 4-2. Charles de Goal, as he was sometimes known, moved to Arsenal – but, of course, he came back again.

19 Jerry Solis, an outside-left who made just nine appearances in season 1931-32 was, in all probability, Celtic's only Jewish player. However, many supporters wrongly assumed that goalkeeper Joe Coen, who was in the side during the same season, was also Jewish.

20 Roman Catholic priests now have to pay to watch Celtic – and that's official! For 110 years priests were not required to pay to watch their beloved team but, since the commencement of the 1996-97 season, they have been required to pay in the usual way. Celtic has replaced this free ticket scheme with a charity scheme for supporters and priests are reportedly pleased, saying that they do not want special privileges.

FOR CLUB AND COUNTRY

Celtic has produced over 120 players who have featured in international matches for the home countries. Of these, by far the greatest number have played for Scotland, but players have also represented the Republic of Ireland and Northern Ireland, while one (reserve keeper Frank Collins, who played his only international against Scotland at Parkhead in March 1922) played for the Irish Free State.

Celtic's two leading internationalists – Packy Bonner and Paul McStay – have a century and a half of appearances between them. Bonner made his international debut for the Republic of Ireland against Poland in 1981 and, even though he was suffering from back trouble, he proved rock solid during the European Nations' Cup in 1988: His performance in the defeat of England at Stuttgart in June of that year will long be remembered. He was also the hero of the day in the World Cup of 1990, when he saved a penalty during the shoot-out with Romania which helped the Republic gain a Quarter-Final place in Rome.

McStay began his international career early, playing for Scotland Schoolboys and, on one occasion, scoring twice in a 5-4 win over England at Wembley. He was skipper of the senior international side for a time and in October 1992, when Scotland played Portugal at Ibrox, he overtook Danny McGrain's then record club total of 62 Scottish caps.

Danny McGrain remains second in the Scottish cap table. His first full international came in 1973 against Wales, his last being against the USSR in 1982. He was made captain of the national side in the summer of 1977, when Kenny Dalglish opted out of a tour of Australasia, and was acclaimed as the best footballer ever seen in Australia – a statement which, in the circumstances, seems hardly surprising.

Dalglish himself comes next on the list. He gained 102 caps in all, but only 47 of these were earned while he was at Celtic – his first being as a substitute against Belgium in 1972. Dalglish is closely followed by Bobby Evans, who played 45 full internationals and also featured in 25 matches for the Scottish League. Full of effort and enthusiasm, half-back Evans' Scottish debut was against England in 1949, his last being against Poland in 1960. He was appointed captain during the World Cup in 1958, but reserved one of his best performances for a game against West Germany at Hampden in May 1959, which Scotland won 3-2.

Chris Morris, Bertie Peacock, Billy McNeill, David Hay and Jimmy Johnstone complete Celtic's top ten on the international front. Morris (34, 1987-92) played for the Republic and did particularly well in the 1990 World Cup; Peacock of Northern Ireland (30, 1952-61) excelled in the World Cup of 1958 and McNeill (29, 1961-72) excelled wherever he went. David Hay (27, 1970-74) did very well in the World Cup at Munich, while Jimmy Johnstone (23, 1965-75), near the end of his international career, had a great game at Hampden against England in May 1974 – only a few days after being rescued from a rowing boat which had allegedly been set adrift by a Rangers player on the Firth of Forth!

WORST SEASON 1

Celtic suffered after the war. When proper football resumed in 1946–47 Rangers won the League Championship, and Celtic finished seventh. To the average supporter this must have seemed like something akin to the end of civilisation but, for the team itself, worse was to follow.

The 1947–48 season saw the side finish in its lowest ever League position – 12th out of 16, in what was then known as the Scottish Division A. There may perhaps have been some small consolation in the fact that Hibs won the title, beating Rangers by a two–point margin, but nothing could disguise the fact that Celtic, in finishing 23 points behind the leaders, had won only ten games and lost 15.

Manager Jimmy McGrory, who had been such a great Celt himself, must have been in despair as he watched his side go down 3–2 at Airdrie on the season's opening day, but perhaps he thought this early result had been merely an aberration when Celtic won the next game, beating Queen's Park 4–0. Not so. Celtic lost the next three, and were clearly in trouble.

Even Willie Miller, an excellent goalkeeper, was unable to stem the tide…although in truth it was often lack of firepower, rather than a poor defence, which hindered Celtic's cause. Only 41 goals were scored and the top marksman, with just seven of them, was Tommy McDonald, playing in his one and only Celtic season. A young Bobby Evans was used in an attacking role for much of the campaign, but he scored only three times, while Frank Walsh and Jock Weir were also largely ineffective – although Weir did score a fine hat-trick at Dundee in a 3-2 win on the last day of the season.

There were one or two notable victories. Partick Thistle were beaten 5-3 at Firhill Park, although Partick won 2-1 at Parkhead; Motherwell went down 3-0 at Fir Park (although they too scored a victory at Parkhead) and Falkirk were beaten 1-0 after (you guessed it) they had inflicted yet another home defeat on the Celts (3-0). It's really quite surprising that Celtic managed to win five of their 15 home fixtures.

Before the final victory at Dundee, Celtic suffered three consecutive defeats, including a 5-1 drubbing at Third Lanark which was followed, a couple of weeks later, by a 3-1 beating by the same side at Parkhead. Third Lanark may be no more, but not many teams can claim to have done the double over Celtic, or to have put them in danger of relegation. That was avoided, but this was definitely a season to forget.

1947-48 LEAGUE RECORD		
Opponents	Home	Away
Aberdeen	1-0	0-2
Airdrieonians	0-0	2-3
Clyde	0-0	0-2
Dundee	1-1	3-2
Falkirk	0-3	1-0
Hearts	4-2	0-1
Hibernian	2-4	1-1
Morton	3-2	0-4
Motherwell	0-1	3-0
Partick Thistle	1-2	5-3
Queen of the South	4-3	0-2
Queen's Park	4-0	2-3
Rangers	0-4	0-2
St Mirren	0-0	2-1
Third Lanark	1-3	1-5

DOUBLE ACTS

One of the earliest and most effective partnerships for Celtic was that of full-backs Donnie McLeod and Jimmy Weir.

McLeod's debut came in a 2-1 win at Third Lanark in a League match played on 30 August 1902, while Weir first appeared at Parkhead in a 1-1 draw with St Mirren on 27 April 1907.

During his first season, McLeod mainly wore the Number 3 shirt, but he switched to right-back during 1903-04. He missed only one League game in the 1904-05 Championship season and featured in the majority of matches when the Championship was again won in both 1905-06 and 1906-07.

Jimmy Weir had made two appearances towards the end of the 1906-07 campaign, but the partnership with McLeod began in earnest with a 3-0 win over Hamilton Academicals in August 1907. It was a partnership which was to last for little more than a season, and yet it is considered to have been one of the most efficient in the history of the club. Perhaps this is hardly surprising, as Celtic conceded only 27 goals in 34 matches on their way to a fourth succesive Championship.

'Slasher' McLeod was a fearless player with a great turn of speed and together with Weir (and with the equally fearless Davy Adams in goal) he formed an almost impenetrable barrier. McLeod was transfered to Middlesbrough in October 1908 and, to the dismay of many a Celtic fan, Weir followed him less than two years later. Their partnership was re-established at Ayresome Park and they were described as the most dogged, dour and fearless pair of backs in England.

Donnie McLeod died from wounds sustained on the Flanders battlefield in October 1917, while Jimmy Weir was still going strong in the 1950s.

Crum and MacDonald were members of the great forward lines of the late 1930s. Johnny Crum made his debut in a 4-1 home win over Motherwell in October 1932, in which he scored twice, while Malky MacDonald first entered the Celtic scene a few months earlier – in a 2-0 win at Partick Thistle where he was the scorer of both goals.

Crum established himself in the League side during the 1933-34 season, while MacDonald gained a regular place as centre-half during 1934-35. It was not until Jimmy McGrory left the scene in 1937 that MacDonald came into his own as a forward.

McGrory's last game was on 16 October, when Queen's Park were beaten 4-3. Jimmy naturally scored one of the goals, but so too did both Crum (wearing 7) and MacDonald (wearing 8) and it was not long before the pair was established as a new strike force. John Divers and Frank Murphy also contributed greatly to the goal tally as Celtic went on to win the 1937-38 League title but, between Christmas Day 1937 and 26 March 1938, Crum and MacDonald between them scored 26 League and Cup goals in 15 matches.

The partnership continued during the last pre-war season. Both scored on the opening day (which was hardly surprising, as Celtic beat Kilmarnock 9-1). MacDonald scored a hat-trick in a 6-2 Old Firm game in September and, a fortnight later, Crum scored three while MacDonald netted twice in a 6-1 beating of Raith Rovers. The next League game proved barren for Malky, but Johnny helped himself to five as Celtic won 8-1 at Albion Rovers.

Jock Stein played against Johnny Crum during the war years, and described him as still a very good and brainy centre-forward. Crum made 211 League and Scottish Cup appearances for Celtic and scored 88 goals. He died in July

1969. MacDonald played 147 League and Cup games, scoring on 37 occasions, and transferred to Kilmarnock at the end of 1945 – afterwards moving to Brentford where he later began a career in management.

Bertie Auld had two spells at Parkhead, and it was during the second of these that he struck up the dynamic partnership with Bobby Murdoch. The early days at Celtic had not always been happy ones for Auld, but not long after his return from Birmingham City in 1965, he scored five in a 6-0 win at Airdrie and, when he followed this up with two goals in the 3-2 defeat of Dunfermline in the Scottish Cup Final, the beginnings of midfield domination by Auld and Murdoch could be seen by one and all.

Celtic were about to begin a run of nine consecutive League Championships and the partnership was to last until 1971. Murdoch wore the Number 4 shirt for most of this period and there were to be some memorable days and nights ahead. Auld was not in the side which won the League Cup final against Rangers (2-1) in 1965, but both were present in the victorious Finals of the two domestic cup competitions, and in the European Cup Final, in 1966-67. They also shared in the glory when the League Cup was won in 1967, 1968, 1969 (where Auld scored the only goal in the Final against St Johnstone) and when the Scottish Cup was again won in 1969 (4-0 v Rangers).

Sean Fallon said of Bertie Auld: 'We were playing mile-a-minute stuff at the time and he complemented Bobby Murdoch by slowing things down. He could take two or three people out of the game with a pass.' Auld and Murdoch would have enjoyed an even longer partnership, but the former was allowed to join Hibernian on a free transfer in May 1971. Murdoch, bored with Scottish football and having won just about everything he could win at Parkhead, later departed for Middlesbrough where he was to make 93 English League appearances.

Bobby Lennox was already well established in the Celtic side – first at outside-left and later in the inside-left position – when Willie Wallace was signed from Hearts in December 1966. Wallace was bought as a likely replacement for Steve Chalmers, but in effect took over from Joe McBride when the latter suffered a serious knee injury shortly after Wallace's arrival at Parkhead. Willie scored twice in a 6-2 win over Partick Thistle in only his second game, and he never looked back until his transfer to Crystal Palace in October 1971.

Both Lennox and Wallace were in the side that won the Scottish Cup Final against Aberdeen in April 1967 (Wallace scored both Celtic's goals in the 2-0 victory) and they were both Lisbon Lions at the end of that extraordinary season. During the 1967-68 League campaign, both achieved a remarkable run of goalscoring. Between 13 and 30 March, Wallace scored nine times (including two hat-tricks) in five games, while between 16 March and 30 April, Lennox scored in nine consecutive matches – 15 goals in all, including four in a 6-1 win at St Johnstone.

Both had scored in the 1967 League Cup Final when Celtic beat Dundee 5-3, and, at the final stage of that competition a year later, Wallace scored one and Lennox netted a hat-trick, as Celtic beat Hibs 6-2. Also in 1968-69, both featured in the 4-0 win over Rangers in the Scottish Cup Final – Lennox scoring one of Celtic's goals. Both played against Rangers in the Scottish Cup Final of 1971 and both featured in the replay (Wallace as sub) when Celtic ran out 2-1 winners.

The speed and fitness Bobby Lennox possessed complemented the mobility and skills of Willie Wallace to tremendous effect.

THROUGH THE YEARS
MAY

1888

May

Celtic Football Club was founded by a group of men eager to provide something that was truly their own for the large Irish-Catholic community of Glasgow. Brother Walfrid is credited with having the idea in the first place, and was aided and abetted by two local businessmen, John McLaughlin and John Glass.

1893

May

18

Celtic lost the last game of the season 5–2 to Third Lanark – but had already won the Scottish League Championship for the first time.

1953

May

20

Celtic won in the Coronation Cup, having beaten both Arsenal and Manchester United to book a place against high-flying Hibs in the Final at Hampden Park. A crowd of over

117,000 witnessed the event and saw Neil Mochan score from 35 yards to give Celtic a half-time lead. Hibernian put Celtic under a great deal of pressure in the second half, but Jimmy Walsh doubled that lead and the Coronation Cup came to Parkhead.

1967
May
13

Danny McGrain signed and was to remain with Celtic for 20 years. Earlier that month Celtic went to Lisbon for the European Cup Final against Inter Milan. Everyone knows the result. The scorers were Gemmell and Chalmers.

1972
May
6

Celtic beat Hibs 6-1 in the Scottish Cup Final. The scorers were Billy McNeill, Dixie Deans (3) and Lou Macari (2). This was not, of course, the only trophy to be won in the merry month of May – the latest being the 1-0 win over Airdrie in 1995, when Pierre van Hooijdonk was the scorer.

1994
May
17

Gary Gillespie, who had cost Celtic £925,000 when bought from Liverpool in 1991, was given a free transfer – apparently to reduce the wage bill.

GREAT MIDFIELDERS

Ball-winners and ball-players have all been instrumental in the Parkhead success story. Here's the history of five midfield marvels.

 ## PATSY GALLAGHER

Patsy Gallagher was born in Ramelton, Co Donegal on 16 April 1893 and was signed for Celtic from Clydebank Juniors by Willie Maley in October 1911. When Maley introduced his new inside-right, Jimmy Quinn remarked: 'If you put that wee thing out on the park, you'll be done for manslaughter, so you will.'

Gallagher was certainly small at about 5 feet 7 inches and weighing in at less than ten stone, but the man from Donegal had remarkable talent. His debut came in a League game against St Mirren in December 1911 which Celtic won 3-1. He scored in his next game, a 4-1 victory at Queen's Park, and soon afterwards established his permanent right to the Number 8 shirt.

Patsy Gallagher scored 196 goals in his Celtic career and was a Northern Ireland international, but his contemporaries often wondered where he got the strength to shoot. He won six League Championship medals from 1914 to 1922 as well as picking up a couple for the Scottish Cup, in 1923 and 1925. He scored a hat-trick against Dumbarton in season 1913–14 and two more, against Ayr United and Partick Thistle, during the following season. Three hat-tricks followed in 1915–16 and in the first game of 1916–17 he went one better, scoring four in a 5–1 drubbing of St Mirren.

Gallagher had made 464 appearances in a Celtic shirt when he was asked to retire in July 1926 following a knee injury. He died in Scotstoun in June 1953.

PATSY GALLGHER CELTIC RECORD 1911-26									
League		FA Cup		League Cup		Europe		Total	
Apps	Goals	Apps	Goals	Apps	Goals	Apps	Goals	Apps	Goals
432	187	32	9	—	—	—	—	464	196

 # JIMMY JOHNSTONE

Outside-right Jimmy Johnstone was born in Viewpark on 30 September 1944. He signed for Celtic in November 1961, having been a ball-boy for three years. Johnstone made his debut in an unhappy 6–0 League defeat at Kilmarnock in March 1963 and he was not Jock Stein's immediate choice for the outside-right slot. However, he came into his own in a League Cup match in 1965 when he played brilliantly to help Celtic to an 8–1 victory over Raith Rovers at Stark's Park.

Johnstone was to become a more or less permanent fixture in the Celtic side over the next few years, although he took a great deal of stick and was prone to retaliation and subsequent sendings-off. He was a ball-playing genius but Stein had his own ideas about what Johnstone should be doing on the field, and there were a number of rows and disagreements.

Jimmy Johnstone had a somewhat flamboyant lifestyle. Stein said that no player had caused him more headaches than the errant 'Jinky' but he probably loved him really. At any rate, he kept bringing him back into the side so he obviously knew he needed him.

Johnstone won 23 Scotland caps and he saved some of his most brilliant Celtic performances for European games. He was a member of the European Cup-winning side of 1967 and, of his total of 515 games, 67 were in European competitions. He won nine Championship medals in a row, four Scottish Cup winner's medals and another four League Cup winner's medals. He later became a Celtic coach under David Hay.

JIMMY JOHNSTONE CELTIC RECORD 1961-75									
League		FA Cup		League Cup		Europe		Total	
Apps	Goals	Apps	Goals	Apps	Goals	Apps	Goals	Apps	Goals
308	82	48	10	92	21	67	16	515	129

 # BOBBY MURDOCH

If ever a player was a manager's favourite, it was Bobby Murdoch. Jock Stein opined: 'His greatest quality is consistency. He turns in one great performance after another and he never fails to give one hundred per cent effort.' After his move to Middlesbrough in September 1973, Jack Charlton said: 'He was my first signing as a manager, and I might never be so lucky again.'

Murdoch was born in Bothwell on 17 August 1944. He signed for Celtic in October 1959 and made his debut in the League Cup against Hearts in August 1962, scoring in a 3–1 victory. Having started life as an attacking player (a philosophy he never really abandoned), he established himself in the right-half position at the commencement of the 1965-66 season and held that place until the end of 1972-73.

He was dropped from the side at the start of season 1973-74, and moved to Middlesbrough. He had made 12 appearances for Scotland and, while with Celtic, he had won eight League Championships, five Scottish Cup and six League Cup medals. He had also earned a European Cup medal and, in 1969, had been voted Scottish Player of the Year. He claimed, however, that he was bored with Scottish football and his move to north-east England would give him the opportunity of a fresh challenge. Celtic therefore lost one of their greatest assets after he had made 484 appearances and scored on 105 occasions.

BOBBY MURDOCH CELTIC RECORD 1959-73									
League		FA Cup		League Cup		Europe		Total	
Apps	Goals	Apps	Goals	Apps	Goals	Apps	Goals	Apps	Goals
291	62	53	13	83	19	57	11	484	105

 # TOMMY BURNS

Glasgow born Tommy Burns came into this world on 16 December 1956. He signed on at Parkhead in August 1973 and made his debut as a substitute in a home League game, which Dundee won 2-1, on 19 April 1975.

'Twists and turns' Burns had true class. He was noted for his tremendous vision and reading of the game and his left foot 'made the ball talk'. He was basically a schemer who created goalscoring opportunites for others, although in his 500 Celtic appearances he himself netted on 81 occasions.

Burns played a number of matches during the 1978-79 season but really established himself in the League side during 1980-81 when he was missing for only four games. His impeccable control led him to the first of eight caps, against Northern Ireland at Hampden Park in May 1981, although this turned out to be one of his less than wonderful games. He did very much better for Celtic in the second leg of the European Cup tie against Sporting Lisbon in November 1983. His side was 2-0 down from the first leg, but Burns was to make a valuable contribution in the second and scored one of the goals in a 5-0 victory.

Tommy Burns won six Championship medals, four Scottish Cup winner's medals and one League Cup winner's medal during his time at Parkhead. He played his last game for Celtic in December 1989 – a friendly against Ajax – and went on to manage Kilmarnock, taking them into the Premier Division in May 1993, before his spell in the Bhoys' hotseat.

TOMMY BURNS CELTIC RECORD 1973-89

League		FA Cup		League Cup		Europe		Total	
Apps	Goals	Apps	Goals	Apps	Goals	Apps	Goals	Apps	Goals
353	52	43	11	70	15	34	3	500	81

 # PAUL McSTAY

Paul McStay, the last in the line of the great Celtic McStay dynasty, was born on 22 October 1964 and became a full professional with the club in February 1981. He made his debut in a Scottish Cup tie versus Queen of the South in January 1981, a game Celtic won 4-0.

McStay began to establish himself in the Championship side of 1981-82 and during the following season was ever-present in the League, Cup and European Cup, featuring in the team which beat Rangers 2-1 in the Final of the League Cup. He continued as a regular in the Number 8 shirt right through until 1994-95.

On occasion, McStay's form was almost unbelievably brilliant. He scored for Celtic, who had been reduced to ten men, near the end of ordinary time in the 1984 Scottish Cup Final against Aberdeen – but, sadly for the Celts, the outfit from Pittodrie were to score the winner in the extra half-hour. At the end of season 1985–86 he scored the fourth goal as Celtic won 5-0 at St Mirren to steal the title from Hearts.

McStay played a vital role during the Centenary Season of 1987–88, playing in every first team game except one (a League Cup encounter at Dumbarton) and steering the side to Double triumph. He became the third member of his family to take over the Celtic captaincy when he replaced Roy Aitken in January 1990, and later also captained the Scottish side.

McStay's fortunes faltered somewhat during 1992–93 and he was not quite the same player after that. He won Championship medals in 1985–86 and 1987–88, Scottish Cup winner's medals in 1985, 1988, 1989 and 1995 and a League Cup winner's medal in 1982–83. The latter part of his career may have been more successful had he not had the resposibilities of captaincy, but it was injury that caused him to call time on a brilliant career in 1997.

In all, Paul McStay MBE made 676 Celtic appearances and scored 70 goals. He also played for his country on 76 occasions, the most of any Celt.

PAUL McSTAY CELTIC RECORD 1981-97									
League		FA Cup		League Cup		Europe		Total	
Apps	Goals	Apps	Goals	Apps	Goals	Apps	Goals	Apps	Goals
514	57	66	6	54	7	42	—	676	70

PLAYER TALK

Footballers use their boots for talking – but these Parkhead favourites put their thoughts into words too!

'To the disgust of my friends at school, I was always mad on Celtic.'

Ally Hunter

'As I walked off Hampden Park I felt I had got everything out of life I had ever wanted. I had become a member of the famous Celtic FC and holder of a Scottish Cup badge all in one year.'

Sean Fallon, following Celtic's triumph over Motherwell in the 1951 Cup Final

'Jimmy Delaney was the greatest inspirational footballer I ever played with or saw. No game was ever lost with Jimmy in the team.'

Johnny Paton

'I've made a reasonable amount of money out here, but my next move has to be with medals in mind, rather than cash.'

Paul Elliott, on his move from Pisa to Celtic in 1989

'When I was a youngster, it was my one and only ambition to play in a green and white jersey. When I was transferred it was one of the greatest disappointments of my life.'

Tommy Docherty

'I'm just glad to be able to say I played for Celtic.'

Alan Rough

'I will be free of the Parkhead terracing critics, of the media guys who wanted me out, of the referees who picked on me.'
Roy Aitken, after his 667 appearances in a Celtic shirt

'Celtic played too much football to suit my game.'
Tony Cascarino

'My job was to look for space and run. Bertie Auld joined Bobby Murdoch in midfield and I was made.'
Bobby Lennox

'In those days people would put an old grey sweatshirt on and train by running round the park and up and down the terracing steps. If people asked for a ball they were told "No, no, no. Patsy Gallagher didn't train with a ball. What was good enough for Patsy is good enough for you".'
John Divers, speaking in the 1950s

'I just want to stay with Celtic. I don't want to go anywhere else. I've always supported Celtic and they are the only club I've wanted to play for.'
Charlie Nicholas in March 1981

'The big problem was getting the breakthrough. As soon as I scored that goal the Italian players' heads went down. They didn't want to know after that. They knew the writing was on the wall.' *Tommy Gemmell, after the European Cup triumph*

'The Championship is the ultimate aim. To win it you've got to do it week in, week out. The weeks that you're not doing that you've still got to grind out the results, even if you're not playing well.'
Paul McStay

THROUGH THE YEARS
JUNE

1895

June

Barney Battles signed for the first time. He was to leave the club in 1897, following his part in a players' revolt (for which he was suspended) but he returned to the fold once more in 1898.

1902

June

6

Jimmy McMenemy signed for Celtic and scored on his League debut against Port Glasgow five months later. He remained at Parkhead until 1920 and died, aged 85, in June 1965.

1948

June

20

Charlie Tully, the miraculous Irishman who dribbled about almost at will, signed. He played for Celtic during some of their unhappier days, but they would have done much worse without him.

1975
June
5

Future Celtic and Scotland skipper Roy Aitken was signed on full professional forms and remained at Parkhead until 1990, when he transferred to Newcastle.

1979
June
18

Mercurial striker Charlie Nicholas signed for the club for the first time. He would wait a year for his League debut but score many goals in Celtic's colours.

1994
June
14

Lou Macari was removed from the seat of management after an uncomfortable spell of less than a year in charge. His playing record between 1967 and 1973 saw him score 57 in 102 appearances for Celtic.

GREAT MATCHES

Celtic have featured in many classic games over their history. We've picked out four as representing their success in three Cup competitions, the League, SFA Cup and European Cup – throwing in a record victory over Rangers for good measure!

> Aberdeen 1 Celtic 2
> 24 April 1937
> Scottish Cup Final

Having won the League title in 1935–36 for the first time in ten years, the next League season was to be something of a disappointment. The Celts could only finish third, but they did reach the Final of the Scottish Cup where League runners-up Aberdeen were to be their opponents.

Cup Finals always attract massive crowds, but none had ever been so large as the one that turned up to witness this particular game. Hampden Park's copious terraces could hold more people than any other British ground, but few could have expected the record attendance of 146,433 – with a further 20,000 locked out.

Willie Buchan was Celtic's best player on the day, his accurate passes splitting open the Dons' defence time and again. Johnny Crum was ever on the lookout for defensive hesitation as Aberdeen nervously attempted to stem the encroaching tide, while Jimmy McGrory, approaching the end of his career and far from fully fit, sold dummies and embarked upon a series of decoy runs.

After just 11 minutes the pressure paid off. A Buchan shot took a deflection and, although Dons keeper Johnstone got a hand to the ball, Crum managed to put it over the line.

Within 60 seconds, however, Aberdeen had rather surprisingly equalised through Armstrong. The goal naturally gave the northern side more confidence and they held on fairly comfortably until half-time. In fact, during the early part of the second period, the Dons exerted increasing pressure on the Celtic defence, but then, with 20 minutes to go, McGrory controlled the ball with his chest and sent the ball into the path of the advancing Buchan. The inside-right shot from 12 yards, the ball hit the foot of the post – and rolled over the line.

There were one or two alarms and excursions before the final whistle, but when it was blown the Celts knew they had won the Cup for the 15th time. They had done it before a record crowd for a domestic match between two European clubs – a record which stands to this day.

Team: Kennaway, Hogg, Morrison, Geatons, Lyon, Paterson, Delaney, Buchan, McGrory, Crum, Murphy.

Celtic 7 Rangers 1
19 October 1957
Scottish League Cup Final

On a sunny autumn afternoon at Hampden Park, as Celtic and Rangers took to the field to contest the League Cup Final, 82,293 fanatical supporters looked forward to another keenly fought Old Firm battle. Two hours later, with the Rangers fans leaving in a state of shock and the Celtic faithful reluctant to leave at all, Scottish footballing history had been made.

Rangers, the reigning Scottish League Champions, started

as favourites, but when Celtic first scored they might already have been ahead. An effort from Charlie Tully struck both posts before being cleared, and Bobby Collins had also been cheated by the woodwork, before Sammy Wilson pounced on a ball headed down by Billy McPhail after 23 minutes.

Collins again hit the woodwork, this time with a free-kick, and McPhail headed against the bar, before Mochan made it 2-0 on the stroke of half-time. His superb shot from a narrow angle followed a run which left both McColl and Shearer stranded, and was a fitting end to a superb 45 minutes.

Play resumed with Celtic having to contend with the sun in their eyes. However, Rangers' Murray had sustained an injury and a hastily reorganised defence allowed McPhail to score his first within ten minutes of the restart. Simpson pulled one back for Rangers three minutes later, but the pattern was established.

McPhail struck again after 68 minutes, his shot ricocheting off the bar and falling perfectly for him to hit the rebound home. Seven minutes later, Mochan made it 5-1 with a stunning left-foot shot, and McPhail completed an historic hat-trick with ten minutes remaining. His third was a classic, as he leapt to head the ball past Valentine and ran round him to collect it before powering forward to beat Niven.

The final twist of the knife came in the last minute. McPhail was brought down but declined the chance to take the penalty and become the first player in an Old Firm game to score four goals. Willie Fernie, whose penetrating runs had done so much to demoralise the Rangers defence, stepped up to make it 7-1.

The match proved to be the last glory day for many Celtic players, but they could have wished for no better memorial. This is undoubtedly the one match no Celtic fan could ever forget, and no Rangers fan will ever be allowed to.

Team: Beattie, Donnelly, Fallon, Fernie, Evans, Peacock, Tully, Collins, McPhail, Wilson, Mochan.

Celtic 2 Inter Milan 1
25 May 1967
European Cup Final

Question: What does Brechin City's Glebe Park ground have in common with the Portuguese National Stadium, as it was in 1967? Answer: Both have neat hedges around part of the ground.

It was to this unusual but elegant stadium that the Celts made their way for the European Cup Final in 1967. A crowd numbering 56,000 (12,000 of them from Glasgow, each of whom had paid between ten shillings and two pounds seven and six for a ticket) were there for the 5.30pm kick-off, and they were to witness Celtic's greatest ever triumph.

Things went badly at first. Jim Craig was adjudged to have brought down Cappellini inside the area after seven minutes, and Mazzola scored from the spot. Inter, however, were a very defensive side and the early lead meant that they all pulled back and allowed Celtic to play. This suited Jock Stein's team of attacking players to perfection, and they proceeded to bombard the Italian defences.

Bombard them they might, but Celtic were still a goal down at half-time. It was a very warm evening and there were fears that the Celts would wear themselves out well before the 90 minutes were up. These fears, however, proved groundless: Jock's men knew they had the beating of Inter and they continued their tactic.

Their reward eventually came. Having had a couple of earlier penalty appeals turned down, an equaliser came in the 63rd minute when Tommy Gemmell accepted a pass from Jim Craig and sent the ball whizzing past goalkeeper Sarti. Gemmell later admitted he shouldn't have been in a position to score, since his right-back partner Craig was already upfield and he should have fallen back to cover.

Italian heads dropped and it was only a matter of time before the winner came. After 85 minutes, Steve Chalmers diverted a low ball from Bobby Murdoch past the stranded Sarti and Celtic became the first British team to lift the premier European trophy.

At least half of Glasgow was really very pleased…

Team: Simpson, Craig, Gemmell, Murdoch, McNeill, Clark, Johnstone, Wallace, Chalmers, Auld, Lennox.

Celtic 3 Dundee United 0
30 November 1997
Scottish Coca-Cola Cup Final

In the great scheme of things this match will certainly not go down as a great one, but it is reported here because it hopefully represents the beginning of a great Celtic revival under the combination of general manager Jock Brown and coach Wim Jansen.

When the Celts stepped out at Ibrox to face Dundee United at the end of November, the League Cup had not been lifted since 1982. Other trophies, too, have been in short supply, so victory over United was essential.

Perhaps overawed at the presence of a Celtic side so clearly determined to win this game, Dundee United were not at their best and the outcome was seldom in doubt. Midway through the first half Morten Wieghorst flighted a perfect cross for Marc Rieper to head home the opening goal and, within a couple of minutes, a Henrik Larsson shot was deflected by Maurice Malpas over the head of keeper Sieb Dijkstra.

The game was virtually over as a contest but, to their credit, Celtic kept up the pressure. They could have had the proverbial hatful, but had to be content with just one more goal – a Craig Burley header in the 59th minute which really did finish United off.

With three central defenders in Boyd, Stubbs and Rieper, and with Mahe, Blinker, McNamara and Thom working hard on the flanks, the main strike force had been left with plenty of room to manoeuvre. It was a satisfying performance and one which promises better times ahead.

Team: Gould, Boyd, Rieper, Stubbs, McNamara (Annoni) Wieghorst, Burley, Blinker (Lambert) Mahe, Larsson, Thom (Donnelly).

LEAGUE CUP RECORD

Introduced just after the war, the
League (currently Coca–Cola) Cup now
resides in the Parkhead trophy room.

Stage	Opponents	Score
1946-47		
Section C	Hibernian	2-4, 1-1
Section C	Third Lanark	0-0, 3-2
Section C	Hamilton A	2-2, 3-1
Celtic failed to qualify for the Quarter-Final		
1947-48		
Section C	Rangers	0-2, 2-0
Section C	Dundee	1-1, 1-4
Section C	Third Lanark	3-1, 2-3
Celtic failed to qualify for the Quarter-Final		
1948-49		
Section A	Hibernian	1-0, 2-4
Section A	Clyde	2-0, 3-6
Section A	Rangers	3-1, 1-2
Celtic failed to qualify for the Quarter-Final		
1949-50		
Section A	Rangers	3-2, 0-2
Section A	Aberdeen	5-4, 1-3
Section A	St Mirren	0-1, 4-1
Celtic failed to qualify for the Quarter-Final		

Stage	Opponents	Score

1950-51

Stage	Opponents	Score
Section A	East Fife	2-0, 1-1
Section A	Third Lanark	2-1, 3-1
Section A	Raith Rovers	2-1, 2-2
Quarter-Final	Motherwell	1-4, 1-0

1951-52

Stage	Opponents	Score
Section A	Third Lanark	1-1, 1-0
Section A	Airdrieonians	1-1, 2-0
Section A	Morton	2-0, 0-2
Quarter-Final	Forfar Athletic	4-1, 1-1
Semi-Final	Rangers	0-3

1952-53

Stage	Opponents	Score
Section A	St Mirren	1-0, 3-1
Section A	Partick Thistle	2-5, 1-0
Section A	Hibernian	1-0, 0-3

Celtic failed to qualify for the Quarter-Final

1953-54

Stage	Opponents	Score
Section B	Aberdeen	0-1, 2-5
Section B	East Fife	1-1, 0-1
Section B	Airdrieonians	1-2, 2-0

Celtic failed to qualify for the Quarter-Final

1954-55

Stage	Opponents	Score
Section D	Falkirk	3-0, 2-2
Section D	Dundee	1-3, 0-1
Section D	Hearts	1-2, 2-3

Celtic failed to qualify for the Quarter-Final

1955-56

Stage	Opponents	Score
Section 4	Queen of the South	4-2, 2-0
Section 4	Falkirk	5-1, 1-1
Section 4	Rangers	4-1, 0-4

Celtic failed to qualify for the Quarter-Final

Stage	Opponents	Score
	1956-57	
Section 2	Aberdeen	2-1, 3-2
Section 2	Rangers	2-1, 0-0
Section 2	East Fife	2-1, 1-0
Quarter-Final	Dunfermline Athletic	6-0, 0-3
Semi-Final	Clyde	2-0
Final	Partick Thistle	0-0, 3-0
	1957-58	
Section 3	Airdrieonians	3-2, 2-1
Section 3	East Fife	4-1, 6-1
Section 3	Hibernian	1-3, 2-0
Quarter-Final	Third Lanark	6-1, 3-0
Semi-Final	Clyde	4-2
Final	Rangers	7-1
	1958-59	
Section 2	Clyde	4-1, 2-0
Section 2	Airdrieonians	3-3, 2-1
Section 2	St Mirren	3-0, 3-6
Quarter-Final	Cowdenbeath	2-0, 8-1
Semi-Final	Partick Thsitle	1-2
	1959-60	
Section 1	Raith Rovers	1-2, 1-0
Section 1	Partick Thistle	1-2, 2-0
Section 1	Airdrieonians	2-4, 2-2
	Celtic failed to qualify for the Quarter-Final	
	1960-61	
Section 2	Third Lanark	2-0, 3-1
Section 2	Partick Thistle	1-1, 1-2
Section 3	Rangers	3-2, 1-2
	Celtic failed to qualify for the Quarter-Final	

Stage	Opponents	Score

1961-62

Section 1	Partick Thistle	3-2, 3-2
Section 1	St Johnstone	0-1, 0-2
Section 1	Hibernian	2-2, 2-1

Celtic failed to qualify for the Quarter-Final

1962-63

Section 2	Hearts	3-1, 2-3
Section 2	Dundee	0-1, 3-0
Section 2	Dundee United	4-0, 0-0

Celtic failed to qualify for the Quarter-Final

1963-64

Section 4	Rangers	0-3, 0-3
Section 4	Kilmarnock	0-0, 2-0
Section 4	Queen of the South	1-1, 3-2

Celtic failed to qualify for the Quarter-Final

1964-65

Section 3	Partick Thistle	0-0, 5-1
Section 3	Hearts	3-0, 6-1
Section 3	Kilmarnock	4-1, 0-2
Quarter-Final	East Fife	0-2, 6-0
Semi-Final	Morton	2-0
Final	Rangers	1-2

1965-66

Section 1	Dundee United	1-2, 3-0
Section 1	Motherwell	1-0, 3-2
Section 1	Dundee	0-2, 3-1
Quarter-Final	Raith Rovers	8-1, 4-0
Semi-Final	Hibernian	2-2, 4-0
Final	Rangers	2-1

Stage	Opponents	Score
1966-67		
Section 4	Hearts	2-0, 3-0
Section 4	Clyde	6-0, 3-1
Section 4	St Mirren	8-2, 1-0
Quarter-Final	Dunfermline Athletic	6-3, 3-1
Semi-Final	Airdrieonians	2-0
Final	Rangers	1-0
1967-68		
Section 2	Dundee United	1-0, 1-0
Section 2	Rangers	1-1, 3-1
Section 2	Aberdeen	3-1, 5-1
Quarter-Final	Ayr United	6-2, 2-0
Semi-Final	Morton	7-1
Final	Dundee	5-3
1968-69		
Section 4	Rangers	2-0, 1-0
Section 4	Morton	4-1, 3-0
Section 4	Partick Thistle	4-0, 6-1
Quarter-Final	Hamilton A	10-0, 4-2
Semi-Final	Clyde	1-0
Final	Hibernian	6-2
1969-70		
Section 1	Airdrieonians	6-1, 3-0
Section 1	Rangers	1-2, 1-0
Section 1	Raith Rovers	5-0, 5-2
Quarter-Final	Aberdeen	0-0, 2-1
Semi-Final	Ayr United	3-3, 2-1
Final	St Johnstone	1-0

Stage	Opponents	Score
	1970-71	
Section 1	Hearts	2-1, 4-2
Section 1	Clyde	5-3, 2-0
Section 1	Dundee United	2-2, 2-2
Quarter-Final	Dundee	2-2, 5-1
Semi-Final	Dumbarton	0-0, 4-3
Final	Rangers	0-1
	1971-72	
Section 4	Rangers	2-0, 3-0
Section 4	Morton	1-0, 0-1
Section 4	Ayr United	3-0, 4-1
Quarter-Final	Clydebank	5-0, 6-2
Semi-Final	St Mirren	3-0
Final	Partick Thistle	1-4
	1972-73	
Section 8	Stirling Albion	3-0, 3-0
Section 8	East Fife	1-1, 3-2
Section 8	Arbroath	5-0, 3-3
Round 2	Stranraer	2-2, 5-2
Quarter-Final	Dundee	0-1, 3-2, 4-1
Semi-Final	Aberdeen	3-2
Final	Hibernian	1-2
	1973-74	
Section 1	Arbroath	2-1, 3-1
Section 1	Falkirk	2-0, 2-1
Section 1	Rangers	2-1, 1-3
Round 2	Motherwell	2-1, 0-1, 3-2
Quarter-Final	Aberdeen	3-2, 0-0
Semi-Final	Rangers	3-2
Final	Dundee	0-1

Stage	Opponents	Score
	1974-75	
Section 4	Motherwell	2-1, 2-2
Section 4	Ayr United	2-3, 5-2
Section 4	Dundee United	1-0, 1-0
Quarter-Final	Hamilton A	2-0, 4-2
Semi-Final	Airdrieonians	1-0
Final	Hibernian	6-3
	1975-76	
Section 3	Aberdeen	1-0, 2-0
Section 3	Hearts	0-2, 3-1
Section 3	Dumbarton	3-1, 8-0
Quarter-Final	Stenhousemuir	2-0, 1-0
Semi-Final	Partick Thistle	1-0
Final	Rangers	0-1
	1976-77	
Section 3	Dundee United	1-0, 1-1
Section 3	Dumbarton	3-0, 3-3
Section 3	Arbroath	5-0, 2-1
Quarter-Final	Albion Rovers	1-0, 5-0
Semi-Final	Hearts	2-1
Final	Aberdeen	1-2
	1977-78	
Round 2	Motherwell	0-0, 4-2
Round 3	Stirling Albion	2-1, 1-1
Quarter-Final	St Mirren	3-1, 2-0
Semi-Final	Hearts	2-0
Final	Rangers	1-2
	1978-79	
Round 1	Dundee	3-1, 3-0
Round 2	Dundee United	3-2, 1-0
Round 3	Motherwell	0-1, 4-1
Quarter-Final	Montrose	1-1, 3-1
Semi-Final	Rangers	2-3

Stage	Opponents	Score
1979-80		
Round 2	Falkirk	2-1, 4-1
Round 3	Stirling Albion	2-1, 2-0
Quarter-Final	Aberdeen	2-3, 0-1
1980-81		
Round 2	Stirling Albion	0-1, 6-1
Round 3	Hamilton A	3-1, 4-1
Quarter-Final	Partick Thistle	1-0, 2-1
Semi-Final	Dundee United	1-1, 0-3
1981-82		
Section 1	St Mirren	1-3, 5-1
Section 1	St Johnstone	0-2, 4-1
Section 1	Hibernian	4-1, 4-1
Celtic failed to qualify for the Quarter-Final		
1982-83		
Section 1	Dunfermline Athletic	6-0, 7-1
Section 1	Alloa	5-0, 4-1
Section 1	Arbroath	3-0, 4-1
Quarter-Final	Partick Thistle	4-0, 3-0
Semi-Final	Dundee United	2-0, 1-2
Final	Rangers	2-1
1983-84		
Round 2	Brechin City	1-0, 0-0
Section 4	Airdrieonians	6-1, 0-0
Section 4	Hibernian	5-1, 0-0
Section 4	Kilmarnock	1-1, 1-0
Semi-Final	Aberdeen	0-0, 1-0
Final	Rangers	2-3
1984-85		
Round 2	Dunfermline Athletic	3-2
Round 3	Airdrieonians	4-0
Quarter-Final	Dundee United	1-2

Stage	Opponents	Score
1985-86		
Round 2	Queen of the South	4-1
Round 3	Brechin City	7-0
Quarter-Final	Hibernian	4-4
Celtic lost 3-4 on penalties		
1986-87		
Round 2	Airdrieonians	2-0
Round 3	Dumbarton	3-0
Quarter-Final	Aberdeen	1-1
Celtic won 4-2 on penalties		
Semi-Final	Motherwell	2-2
Celtic won 5-4 on penalties		
Final	Rangers	1-2
1987-88		
Round 2	Forfar Athletic	3-1
Round 3	Dumbarton	5-1
Quarter-Final	Aberdeen	0-1
1988-89		
Round 2	Ayr United	4-1
Round 3	Hamilton A	7-2
Quarter-Final	Dundee United	0-2
1989-90		
Round 2	Dumbarton	3-0
Round 3	Queen of the South	2-0
Quarter-Final	Hearts	2-2
Celtic won 3-1 on penalties		
Semi-Final	Aberdeen	0-1

Stage	Opponents	Score

1990-91

Stage	Opponents	Score
Round 2	Ayr United	4-0
Round 3	Hamilton A	1-0
Quarter-Final	Queen of the South	2-1
Semi-Final	Dundee United	2-0
Final	Rangers	1-2

1991-92

Round 2	Morton	4-2
Round 3	Raith Rovers	3-1
Quarter-Final	Airdrieonians	0-0

Celtic lost 2-4 on penalties

1992-93

Round 2	Stirling Albion	3-0
Round 3	Dundee	1-0
Quarter-Final	Hearts	2-1
Semi-Final	Aberdeen	0-1

1993-94

Round 2	Stirling Albion	2-0
Round 3	Arbroath	9-1
Quarter-Final	Airdrieonians	1-0
Semi-Final	Rangers	0-1

1994-95

Round 2	Ayr United	1-0
Round 3	Dundee	2-1
Quarter-Final	Dundee United	1-0
Semi-Final	Aberdeen	1-0
Final	Raith Rovers	2-2

Celtic lost 5-6 on penalties

1995-96

Round 2	Ayr United	3-0
Round 3	Raith Rovers	2-1
Quarter-Final	Rangers	0-1

Stage	Opponents	Score
	1996-97	
Round 2	Clyde	3-1
Round 3	Alloa	5-1
Quarter-Final	Hearts	0-1
	1997-98	
Round 2	Berwick Rangers	7-0
Round 3	St Johnstone	1-0
Quarter-Final	Motherwell	1-0
Semi-Final	Dunfermline Athletic	1-0
Final	Dundee United	3-0

League Cup Record Club By Club

Opposition	P	W	D	L	F-A
Aberdeen	25	12	4	9	38-33
Airdrieonians	20	13	5	2	45-18
Albion Rovers	2	2	—	—	6-0
Alloa	3	3	—	—	14-2
Arbroath	9	8	1	—	36-8
Ayr United	12	10	1	1	39-13
Berwick Rangers	1	1	—	—	7-0
Brechin City	3	2	1	—	8-0
Clyde	12	11	—	1	37-14
Clydebank	2	2	—	—	11-2
Cowdenbeath	2	2	—	—	10-1
Dumbarton	9	7	2	—	32-8
Dundee	19	10	2	7	37-26
Dundee United	22	12	5	5	32-19
Dunfermline Athletic	8	7	—	1	32-10
East Fife	12	7	3	2	27-11
Falkirk	8	6	2	—	15-5
Forfar Athletic	3	2	1	—	14-5
Hamilton A	10	9	1	—	40-11
Hearts	17	11	1	5	39-22
Hibernian	20	10	5	5	50-34
Kilmarnock	6	3	2	1	8-4
Montrose	2	1	1	—	4-2
Morton	9	7	—	2	23-7
Motherwell	15	9	3	3	26-19
Partick Thistle	21	13	3	5	45-23
Queen of the South	7	6	1	—	18-7
Raith Rovers	11	8	2	1	35-12
Rangers	40	18	2	20	59-59
St Johnstone	6	3	—	3	6-6
St Mirren	13	10	—	3	37-16
Stenhousemuir	2	2	—	—	3-0
Stirling Albion	10	8	1	1	24-5
Stranraer	2	1	1	—	7-4
Third Lanark	12	9	2	1	28-11

THE BOSS FILES

The Celtic manager's job used to be one that needed stamina – the likes of Maley and Stein made themselves fixtures in the Parkhead boss's office thanks to their success. The turnover's been rather greater in recent years, but the supremo's seat still remains one of the most coveted in football. We profile all those who've occupied it with 'boot' ratings out of five.

Willie Maley
1897–1940

Honours: Division One Champions

Division One Champions	1892-93, 1893-94, 1895-96, 1897-98, 1904-05, 1905-06, 1906-07, 1907-08, 1908-09, 1909-10, 1913-14, 1914-15, 1915-16, 1916-17, 1918-19, 1921-22, 1925-26, 1935-36, 1937-38
FA Cup Winners	1891-92, 1898-99, 1899-1900, 1903-04, 1906-07, 1907-08, 1910-11, 1911-12, 1913-14,

| | 1922–23, 1924–25, 1926–27, 1930–31, 1932–33, 1936–37 |
| FA Cup Runners-up | 1888–89, 1892–93, 1893–94, 1900–01, 1901–02, 1925–26, 1927–28 |

Many a football manager today would be happy to be told that he would last half a dozen seasons with a club, but Willie Maley held the job at Celtic for an incredible 43 years.

There was, perhaps, rather less pressure on managers then and the job was certainly very different from the one managers are expected to do today, but Maley must have been very good at what he did. He had a talent for selecting youngsters from the junior ranks and turning them into solid professionals, and the results speak for themselves.

He was a somewhat strict gentleman but clearly knew how to get the best from his players. In his later years he hardly ever watched his team play and was frequently at odds with his chairman, who forced him into retirement at the age of 71! He did not want to go, however, and bore a grudge for many years. Maley died in 1958, aged 89.

Jimmy McStay
1940–45
Honours: None
A legendary former player, McStay became Celtic's manager having gained previous experience with Bridville (Dublin) and Alloa Athletic. Unfortunately, when he arrived back at Parkhead there was a war on, and more unfortunately still, nobody at the club was taking wartime football very seriously. There was little the new manager could do and he was to depart before the re-commencement of serious hostilities on the field.

Jimmy McGrory
1945–65

Honours:
Division One Champions	1953–54	
FA Cup Winners	1950–51, 1953–54	
FA Cup Runners-up	1954–55, 1955–56,	
	1960–61, 1962–63	
League Cup Winners	1955–56, 1956–57,	
	1957–58	
League Cup Runners-up	1964–65	

The greatest goalscorer in the history of British football was destined to have rather less success as a manager. Celtic were almost relegated in 1948, but things improved thereafter. They would probably have got a great deal better had McGrory always been allowed to pick the side, but this rather important task was often undertaken by chairman Bob Kelly who had some strange ideas about team selection.

However, some very good players were brought in during this period – Bobby Collins and Bertie Peacock among them – and there were one or two notable triumphs, particularly the 7-1 defeat of Rangers in the 1957 League Cup Final.

Early in 1965 McGrory abandoned his managerial post in favour of a job as Celtic's public relations officer. He stayed with the club for 14 more years and died in 1982, aged 78.

Jock Stein
1965–78

Honours: Division One Champions   1965–66, 1966–67,
                                                            1967–68, 1968–69,
                                                            1969–70, 1970–71,
                                                            1971–72, 1972–73,
                                                            1973–74

Premier Division Champions	1976–77
FA Cup Winners	1964–65, 1966–67, 1968–69, 1970–71, 1971–72, 1973–74, 1974–75, 1976–77
FA Cup Runners–up	1965–66, 1969–70, 1972–73
League Cup Winners	1965–66, 1966–67, 1967–68, 1968–69, 1973–74
League Cup Runners–up	1970–71, 1971–72, 1972–73, 1973–74, 1974–75, 1975–76, 1976–77, 1977–78
European Cup Winners	1966–67
European Cup Runners–up	1969–70

Jock Stein lived and breathed football. Following managerial success at Dunfermline and Hibs, he took up the reins at Parkhead in March 1965 and led Celtic to some unprecedented triumphs.

He had been Celtic's reserve-team coach in the late 1950s and as such was instrumental in bringing on the likes of Bertie Auld and Pat Crerand, but now it was time to begin achieving in earnest. The trophy cabinet groaned under the weight of silverware as the club won nine consecutive League titles, plus a Premier Division crown. They also won the Scottish Cup eight times and the League Cup on six occasions – and, of course, the European Cup in 1967.

Stein missed the 1975–76 season following a car crash which almost cost him his life, but he returned to the trophy hunt a year later. He left to manage Leeds United at the end of the 1977–78 season but, a few weeks later, resigned to take charge of the Scotland side. He died, aged 62, in September 1985, having just seen the national team beat Wales at Ninian Park.

Sean Fallon
1975–76

Long-time Celtic servant Sean Fallon took over from Jock Stein for ten months, following Stein's road accident in the summer of 1975. No major honours were won during the season.

Billy McNeill
1978–83, 1987–91

Honours: Premier Division Champions 1978–79, 1980–81, 1981–82, 1987–88

FA Cup Winners   1979–80, 1987–88, 1988–89

FA Cup Runners–up   1989–90

League Cup Winners   1982–83

League Cup Runners–up   1990–91

Billy McNeil was the natural choice to succeed Jock Stein. The former Celts captain had enjoyed outstanding success as a player and was to do very well as the manager at Parkhead. Silverware stocks increased but McNeil did not get on with chairman Desmond White and headed south for Manchester City in the summer of 1983. He then took over at Aston Villa and was sacked when they were relegated, but returned to Celtic. Billy McNeill was still highly thought of as a manager, adding a League and two Cups to his roll of honour, but this did not stop him from being given the order of the boot in 1991 following a loss of form by the Celtic side.

David Hay
1983–87

Honours: Premier Division Champions 1985-86
FA Cup Winners 1984-85
FA Cup Runners-up 1983-84
League Cup Runners-up 1983-84, 1985-86

David Hay was not too certain about taking the job at Celtic. The managerial chair's previous occupants had not been well treated by the directors and he had just secured himself a job in Florida.

He accepted the challenge, however, and guided the club to the runners-up positions in all three domestic competitions in his first season in charge. This, of course, was hardly good enough for Celtic, but things soon improved, with the Scottish Cup being won in 1985 and the Championship the following year.

Hay lost his job after a home defeat by Falkirk at the end of the 1986-87 season. To make matters worse (far worse) Rangers had won the Championship, and so it was deemed appropriate that the Celtic boss should seek alternative employment.

Liam Brady
1991–93

Honours: None

Brady's appointment as manager in June 1991 was controversial, in that he was the first manager not to have spent at least some of his playing days at the club. Born in Dublin, he had enjoyed success with Arsenal, Juventus and Inter Milan but this success was destined not to be repeated at Parkhead.

During 1991-92 Celtic lost both home League games against Rangers (although they did secure a draw and a win at Ibrox) and also lost 5-1 to unfancied Neuchatel Xamax in the UEFA Cup. They finished the League campaigns of 1991-92 and 1992–93 in third place and failed to win either cup competition. In October 1993 Brady decided to call it a day, and offered his resignation – which was duly accepted.

Lou Macari
1993–94
Honours: None

Lou Macari's tenure was shorter, and even less successful, than that of Liam Brady. He was appointed in October 1993 and was sacked by Fergus McCann, the newly appointed managing director, in June 1994.

Celtic had finished 1993–94 in fourth place and Macari had dispensed with the services of four centre forwards. The side had failed to qualify for a place in any European competition in 1994–95, while their manager had, in the eyes of some, failed to show sufficient commitment by continuing to live mainly in Stoke on Trent. Macari had to go.

Tommy Burns
1994–97
Honours: FA Cup Winners   1994–95

         League Cup Runners-up   1994–95

Tommy Burns was appointed in July 1994 and charged with restoring the fortunes of Celtic Football Club. He very nearly made a significant impression early in his first season, as his side reached the final of the Scottish Coca-Cola Cup, only to lose on penalties to First Division Raith Rovers.

Playing their home games at Hampden Park while Parkhead was undergoing redevelopment, the Bhoys endured a very moderate League season, finishing fourth. However, a trophy was finally secured at the season's end when Pierre Van Hooijdonk scored against Airdrieonians to bring home the Scottish Cup.

Burns' early success was not built upon. Shortly before the end of the 1996–97 League season, with his side about to finish in the runners-up position, he departed. He is now serving under Kenny Dalglish at Newcastle.

Wim Jansen
1997–

Honours: League Cup Winners   1997-98

Dutchman Wim Jansen is the latest in the line of manager/coaches to take charge at Celtic, although he is working under the general managership of Jock Brown. Jansen, too, was appointed in an attempt to revive the club's fortunes, and he has already had some success. Using three central defenders (Boyd, Stubbs and Rieper), he guided Celtic to a 3-0 win over Dundee United in the 1997-98 Scottish Coca-Cola (League) Cup Final. But of course, his real test is yet to come.

BEST SEASON 2

When Celtic embarked upon the 1935–36 season, it had been nine long years since they had won the Championship.

The first match of the new campaign was at Aberdeen…and when the Celts came away with just one Jimmy McGrory goal to put against the three scored by the home side, even more doom and gloom was forecast. Against all odds, however, this was to prove Celtic's best League season for many years. McGrory scored in each of the first eight games, which included a 6-0 victory over Third Lanark, a 4-0 win over Albion Rovers and a 5-3 defeat of Dunfermline. These games provided McGrory with three hat-tricks, but he missed a couple before returning to score in each of the next six. In fact, Jimmy would fail to score in only four of the League games in which he featured that season.

In a generally high-scoring season (Celtic had the ball in the net on 115 occasions, while Rangers scored 110 times and Aberdeen 96), the Celts conceded only 33 times − keeper Kennaway maintaining clean sheets on 14 occasions and his deputy, James Fox Foley, maintaining a further four.

Right-back Bobby Hogg was ever present, as was skipper and centre-half Willie Lyon, and the remaining defensive duties were mainly shared by Willie McGonagle, Jock Morrison, Chic Geatons and George Paterson.

McGrory simply couldn't stop scoring, and between 21 December and 18 April he netted another four hat-tricks. He was aided and abetted by inside-forward Willie Buchan, who had almost signed for Rangers in 1933. Buchan was another ever-present in this superb Celtic side, and he added 11 goals of his own, while Frank Murphy − who scored one of the two goals at Ibrox, as Celtic recorded their first victory there for many years – netted 13 times.

Outside-right Jimmy Delaney (18 goals) and Johnny Crum (8) completed the attack, and there were also contributions from Willie Fagan (3), Willie Hughes (2) and John McInally (1). Delaney was to make a career total of 160 League and Cup appearances for Celtic, scoring 73 goals, while Crum played 211 times, scoring on 88 occasions.

The 1935–36 season finished with Celtic on 66 points, gained from 38 matches (two points for a win, one for a draw). They had won 32 games and been beaten just four times, by Aberdeen on that very first day of the season, and by Dunfermline, Rangers (at Parkhead) and Hearts. Their biggest wins were over Third Lanark and Ayr United, both 6-0, and they scored five on a further six occasions.

1935–36 LEAGUE RECORD

Opponents	Home	Away
Aberdeen	5-3	1-3
Airdrieonians	4-0	3-2
Albion Rovers	4-0	3-0
Arbroath	5-0	2-0
Ayr United	6-0	2-0
Clyde	2-1	4-0
Dundee	4-2	2-0
Dunfermline	5-3	0-1
Hamilton Academicals	1-0	2-0
Hearts	2-1	0-1
Hibernian	4-1	5-0
Kilmarnock	4-0	1-1
Motherwell	5-0	2-1
Partick Thistle	1-1	3-1
Queen of the South	3-1	5-0
Queen's Park	3-0	3-2
Rangers	3-4	2-1
St Johnstone	2-0	3-2
Third Lanark	6-0	3-1

THE GROUNDS

Recent years have, for a variety of reasons, seen many clubs move to new locations. Celtic, however, have moved no more than a couple of hundred yards from the site of their first pitch in Glasgow's East End since the formation of the club in 1888.

The city's large Irish–Catholic population, although poor and often despised, freely gave of its time and energy to build the original stadium. This was all the more remarkable given that paid employment, when it was available, involved long hours and very low wages. Nevertheless, the club built its own ground, complete with a stand, changing rooms and terracing moulded from the earth already on the site – and did almost all of it with voluntary labour. Celtic's first match at the ground was against Rangers, and resulted in a 5-2 home win. Admission was sixpence, although women were allowed in without payment.

Celtic moved in 1892, when the club's landlord tried to raise the rent from £50 to £450 per annum. The site of the new ground, just across Janefield Street, was a flooded brickfield needing massive amounts of transported earth to turn it into anything like a football stadium. Once again, the local community came to the rescue with its voluntary labour and began to construct a ground which would be fit for the finest team in Scotland. This led to Parkhead earning its nickname when a supporter, reflecting on the move from the old ground near to the Eastern Necropolis (large cemetery) noted, 'It's like moving from the graveyard to Paradise.'

In 1894 the club provided the first press box to be installed at a football ground, thus enabling correspondents of the day to practice their art in comparative comfort, although mobile phones came later. The Grant Stand was built in 1899 and was quite a feature in its day, but it was not very popular with the late Victorian and Edwardian fans as poor ventilation caused the windows to steam up.

Over the years Parkhead has been used for speedway racing, boxing matches and religious meetings. It was also used for cycle racing and it was the proposed construction of a cement cycle track which led the Celtic committee to decide that the club should be turned into a limited company, buying the ground from the landlord for what was, at the time, the considerable sum of £10,000.

Over the next few decades a number of improvements were made. The Grant Stand, which had been ahead of its time even though nobody could see out of it, had disappeared by the end of the 1920s, and in 1929 a new main stand was erected.

Floodlights came late to Parkhead. They did not light up the Jungle until October 1959, when Wolverhampton Wanderers were the victorious visitors for the official switching-on, but it is believed that Celtic played Clyde under some form of floodlighting way back in 1893. The 1959 floodlights were excellent, and were to help Celtic light up Europe within a very few years.

At the beginning of the 1994–95 season Celtic Football Club left the ground which had been its home for 102 years – but the absence would not be for long. With the help of money raised through the share issue, Celtic Park was to be largely rebuilt and converted into a magnificent all-seater stadium, a North Stand seating 26,000 spectators being opened in August 1995. With the old place now unrecognisable, one wonders what those early volunteers would have thought of it all…

THROUGH THE YEARS
JULY

1944
July
23

With the war not yet over, Bobby Evans signed a week after his 17th birthday. He was to be at the club for almost 16 years.

1966
July
21

Pocket–size striker Lou Macari signed for Celtic and went on to score 57 goals in 102 games before moving to Manchester United in 1973.

1991
July
8

After a dispute over alleged breach of contract, defender Paul Elliott left for Chelsea. He had been at Celtic for just two years, having signed on 3 July 1989 following a spell of Italian football with Pisa.

1994
July
12

Tommy Burns took over as manager. He hoped for money to be made quickly available for the purchase of new players but, even though he did buy Andy Walker, Phil O'Donnell and – eventually – Pierre van Hooijdonk, his hopes were to be largely unfulfilled.

1995
July
28

Celtic sign German international striker Andreas Thom from Bayer Leverkusen for £2.2 million. A near-namesake, James Thom, had played a single game for the Bhoys in 1895.

ATTENDANCES

Large crowds have been a feature of games involving Celtic down the years. As early as April 1904, a then record crowd of 65,323 for a Scottish Cup match saw the Celts beat Rangers 3-2 in the Final, with Jimmy Quinn scoring a hat-trick.

Unfortunately, when the same two clubs met at the Semi-Final stage almost a year later, a section of the large crowd invaded the pitch towards the end with Celtic 2-0 down, and the referee was forced to abandon the match – which was later awarded to Rangers.

Even during the 1890s massive crowds flocked to see Celtic games, an example being the first attempt to stage the Cup final of 1892. The Bhoys were to play Queen's Park at Ibrox and 40,000 got in – with another 20,000 locked out. Again there were frequent pitch invasions and although the game was finished, with Celtic winning by the only goal, it was replayed a month later. This time admission prices were doubled to two shillings, and only 23,000 of the slightly less poverty-stricken fans saw Celtic win 5-1.

Celtic have set crowd records at many an away ground, but figures for attendances, especially during the earlier years, are not always reliable. There can be no doubt that from the very beginning gates ran into thousands, but nobody was obliged to report accurate figures and, in any case, fans quite often effected entrance by nefarious means – in other words, they got in for nothing. This even happened at Hampden in 1970, when Celtic played Leeds United in the second leg of the

European Cup Semi-Final. A European Cup record of 136,505 was registered, but a gate was broken down and quite a few non-paying guests got to see Celtic win 2-1.

There were 146,433 fans at the Cup Final against Aberdeen in 1937 (2-1 to the Bhoys) but again a few Celtic fans showed the strength of their support by demolishing some hardware. A few months later, on Ne'erday (1 January) 1938, the largest attendance at Parkhead (92,000) was recorded, and those present witnessed a 3-0 win over Rangers. It is now believed, however, that this figure was an exaggeration. Old Firm games have always attracted enormous crowds, the League Cup Final of 1966 being a prime example, when 94,532 saw Celtic win 1-0.

On the continent, there were 85,000 present in the Ukraine to see Dynamo Kiev win 2-1 in the European Cup (September 1967), 81,000 for the European Cup Quarter-Final in Milan (March 1969 – Celtic lost 1-0) and 75,000 at both the home and away games when Celtic played out two goalless draws with Inter in the Semi-Finals of the European Cup in 1971-72. Again in the European Cup, this time in 1973-74, Parkhead admitted 71,000 fans for the second leg of the Quarter-Final against Basle. Celtic were 3-2 down from the first leg, but won the second game 4-2 in extra time. This tie was followed by the infamous first leg of the Semi-Final at Atletico Madrid, where 75,000 people saw a 0-0 draw, three Spaniards sent off and nine players booked.

Even Celtic have attracted a low gate. During the 1890s the crowd for a game against Abercorn may have failed to reach four figures, but this seems to have been an isolated incident caused more by appalling weather than lack of interest. In the main, the crowds have always turned out and there is perhaps no more remarkable figure than the 40,000 who turned out after the European Cup triumph to watch the triumphant Celtic players parade around Parkhead in a lorry.

DREAM TEAM 2

This side, the legendary Lisbon Lions, simply won everything in 1966-67 – League Cup, the Scottish Cup, League Championship and European Cup.

Goalkeeper   **Ronnie Simpson**

Simpson, who seldom made a mistake, was between the posts for 58 of the 59 matches played that season, and conceded a mean 48 goals in all.

Right-back   **Jim Craig**

Craig, a dentist by profession, was an outstanding athlete who should have won more than a single Scotland cap.

Left-back   **Tommy Gemmell**

Gemmell scored 64 goals in his Celtic career, including 31 from the penalty spot. He also scored in Lisbon and Stein called him the best left-back in the world.

Right-half   **Bobby Murdoch**

Missed only five games all season and was a typical tower of strength.

Centre-half   **Billy McNeill**

'Caesar' missed just one game and needless to say hoisted all four Cups aloft as captain.

Left-half   **John Clark**
Under Jock Stein, Clark had established himself as a fine
sweeper and was ever-present.

Outside-right   **Jimmy Johnstone**
He scored twice at Ibrox to secure the draw which gave Celtic
the Championship, and less than three weeks later he, along
with the rest, was playing his heart out at Lisbon.

Inside-right   **Willie Wallace**
Did not play for the entire season but scored two vital goals at
Parkhead in the European Cup Semi-Final (first leg) against
Dukla Prague to help seal the trip to the Final. He also scored
the two goals which beat Aberdeen in the Final of the
Scottish Cup.

Centre-forward   **Steve Chalmers**
Substitute for the League Cup Final against Rangers, he came
on for John Hughes. Chalmers was one of the game's
gentlemen and he later gave Hughes his winner's medal. He
scored what is widely regarded as Celtic's most important goal
five minutes from time in Lisbon, and he netted 34 times
altogether in 1966-67.

Inside-left   **Bertie Auld**

A major factor during the season of seasons, Auld managed to keep his temperament under control for most of the campaign (he had once laid out England's Johnny Haynes) and gave one of his best ever performances in the European Cup Final.

Outside-left   **Bobby Lennox**

Nicknamed 'Lemon', he scored 24 times in a season which, for him, comprised 45 games.

CFC TRIVIA QUIZ

Test your Parkhead knowledge.
Answers on page 190-191.

1   In which year was Celtic formed?

2   In which British city did Jock Stein die?

3   Can you name the Celtic goalkeeper who died after a game against Rangers in 1931?

4   What was the score when Celtic beat Dundee United in the Scottish Coca-Cola Cup Final in 1997?

5   Name the scorers in that game.

6   What was Bertie Peacock's real first name?

7   Who took over from Willie Maley as manager in February 1940?

8   Who took over from Roy Aitken as Celtic skipper in January 1990?

9   Who became Celtic's skipper in September 1923?

10   After which England goalkeeper did Celtic keeper Gordon Marshall name his son?

11   Who scored the only goal of the 1995 Scottish Cup Final?

12   Who was known as Charles de Goal?

13   In total, how many first-team appearances did Billy McNeill make for Celtic – 97, 790 or 970?

14   In which year were floodlights installed at Parkhead?

15   Who was known as the Wee Rhino?

16   Which Celtic player grew a beard to celebrate being made Scotland's Player of the Year in 1977?

17   To which English club did Brian McClair move in July 1987?

18   From which club did Celtic sign Paul Elliott in 1989?

19   Owen made 87 appearances for Celtic during the 1980s, and was obviously a churchman. What is his surname?

20   Barney was often in the wars and played for Celtic between 1895 and 1904. He died in 1905. Can you put a surname to him?

21   Neither Pat nor Packy, this keeper made 180 appearances for Celtic in the 1950s – name him.

22   What was the score when Celtic thrashed Rangers in the 1957 League Cup Final?

23   Who scored a hat-trick in that game?

24 Three players called Divers have played for Celtic. What were their Christian names?

25 Four players called Docherty have played for Celtic. Two of them were called Jimmy – what were the other two called?

26 What was Bobby Evans' nickname?

27 Who scored eight goals for Celtic against Dunfermline in 1928?

28 Which English club did Steve Fulton join when he left Celtic in July 1993?

29 Ally Hunter kept goal for Celtic on 91 occasions. In how many of these games did he prevent the ball from entering the net – 28, 36 or 43?

30 Name the five clubs former player Lou Macari has managed.

31 At the end of which season did Celtic find themselves Scottish League Champions for the first time?

32 When, pre-1997-98, did Celtic last win the Championship?

33 Celtic beat Arbroath 9-1 in a League Cup tie in August 1993. Name the player who came on as sub and scored a hat-trick.

34 What was Dariusz Dziekanowski's nickname?

35 What was Dariusz Wdowczyck's nickname?

36 How many goals did Celtic concede on their way to the European Cup Final in 1966–67?

37 Celtic were runners–up for the Premier Division title in 1996–97. Who came third?

38 Who is Celtic's most capped player?

39 Which team beat Celtic 8–0 in a League match in April 1937?

40 What was the score when Celtic beat Dundee by a record margin in 1895?

THROUGH THE YEARS
AUGUST

1890
August

Was Celtic's first Scottish League match against Renton, or was it against Hearts? It depends how you look at it. The League kicked off for the first time on 16 August 1890 and Celtic's Parkhead opponents were Renton. A crowd of 10,000 turned out to see the fixture and Renton, who had previously described themselves as champions of the world because they had defeated English Cup holders West Bromwich Albion, won 4-1.

However, Renton were later expelled from the League and the matches in which they had taken part were declared void. So Celtic's second game, a 5-0 win at Hearts on the 23rd, officially became their first League encounter – which, after all, is much more satisfactory.

1931
August

Celtic played six League games in August, and scored 23 goals. There were wins over Leith Athletic (3-0), Dundee United (3-2), Heart of Midlothian (3-0), Cowdenbeath (7-0) and Hamilton Academicals (6-1), and there was a 1-1 draw at Aberdeen. Jimmy McGrory scored 11 of the goals, including four against the boys frae near Lochgelly and a hat-trick against the Accies.

1977
August
10

Kenny Dalglish left for Liverpool. Jock Stein was reportedly very upset and was himself to depart within the year.

1992
August
14

Full-back Rudi Vata became the first Albanian to play British professional football when he joined Celtic. He signed on the same day as Andy Payton and Stuart Slater, and is enigmatically quoted as having said: 'I was signed as a centre-half, but Mr Brady told me I would need to speak English better before I could play there.'

1995
August
5

The new North Stand was officially opened. Rod Stewart cut the tape and John Collins scored from the penalty spot as Celtic played a friendly match against Newcastle United.

TRANSFERS

When Celtic was founded, the idea was to build a team to rival the best in Scotland, but the founding fathers soon discovered that this was easier said than done.

E ven in the 1890s good players were scarce and it was necessary to be on the lookout for fresh talent. In theory, footballers were amateurs, but Celtic became renowned for offering incentives and poaching players. Together with John Glass, Willie Maley would turn up at the homes of unsuspecting players to persuade them to join. More than the odd bawbee would change hands and, to the annoyance of the Scottish FA (not to mention the teams involved), the outcome would often be a new pair of legs in Paradise.

With the recognition of professionalism, things settled down a bit and official transfers started to take place. An early example was the purchase of Jimmy Hay from Ayr in 1903, when the princely sum of £50 changed hands. Eight years later Celtic sold the left-half to Newcastle for £1,250.

Transfer fees remained very low by today's standards for a long time, and Celtic never liked to pay out a great deal. They were however somewhat astute when it came to selling players. In 1923 they managed to unload the temperamental Jock Gilchrist to Preston for a remarkable £4,500 – a purchase Preston later regretted. Four years later Maley dug deep to find the £30 necessary to buy left-back Tom Sinclair from Alva Albion Rangers, and must have been truly mortified when Sinclair failed to make the grade and was allowed to depart for South Shields.

After the war, Celtic were a little more free with their money. Outside-right Jock Weir cost £7,000 from Blackburn in 1948 while, 25 years later, Celtic paid Kilmarnock £40,000 for goalkeeper Ally Hunter (a week after Jock Stein had sold Lou Macari to Manchester United for £200,000). Graeme Sinclair came from Dumbarton for £65,000 in 1982, while Brian McClair was signed from Motherwell a year later for £75,000. Sinclair was allowed to go free in 1985, but McClair was sold to Manchester United in 1987 for £850,000. Charlie Nicholas went to Arsenal in 1983 for a fee of £650,000 (returning in 1990, after a stint with Aberdeen) and Mike Galloway cost £500,000 from Hearts in June 1989.

The number of transfers then increased as Celtic endeavoured to return to the glory trail. John Collins, whom Celtic had missed out on signing earlier, cost £1 million when he came from Hibs in 1990, and Tony Cascarino cost £1.1 million when Liam Brady signed him from Aston Villa in July 1991. A month later Gary Gillespie came from Liverpool for £925,000. He was released in 1994 during a period of financial crisis.

Rudi Vata cost a mere £200,000 when he came from Dinamo Tirana in 1992. Pat McGinlay was bought in July 1993 for £525,000, but Hibs bought him back again in November 1994, for £420,000. Lee Martin was out of contract at Manchester United when Celtic bought him for £350,000 in January 1994, while Andy Walker, when he returned to Celtic Park from Bolton in June 1994, cost £550,000 – although Bolton had wanted £2.2 million.

Recent arrivals from the Continent have cost something or nothing depending on the Bosman ruling. Defenders Marc Rieper and Alan Stubbs have both been big-money buys, the latter £4.2 million in 1996. Tommy Johnson, like Stubbs lured north of the border to join a footballing giant by Tommy Burns, was made open to offers less than a year after his £2.3 million move from Aston Villa.

WORST SEASON 2

The 1959-60 season was another in which Celtic lost more games than they won. This time Hearts were to finish on top of the table, four points ahead of Kilmarnock – Celtic finishing a disappointing ninth.

Rangers had won the title in the previous season, Celtic finishing sixth in a division consisting of 18 clubs, and everyone at Parkhead thought an improvement in fortune was long overdue. But the Celtic faithful would have to wait a wee while yet.

The campaign began brightly enough with a 2-0 win at the home of eventual runners-up Kilmarnock, but this was followed by a 3-1 defeat at Ibrox and another – this time by four goals to three – at home to Hearts. Early season victories at Arbroath (5-0) and over Motherwell (5-1) helped steady the nerves, but Celtic were still quite obviously far from their best.

Frank Haffey had replaced Dick Beattie as first-choice goalkeeper, and he did well enough. Haffey was later to suffer the indignity of being between the Scottish posts for the 9-3 humiliation by England at Wembley, but for now he contented himself with saving a Billy Little penalty in the home fixture with Rangers. He did brilliantly, but Rangers still won 1-0. The defence was to concede a total of 59 goals all told, even though Duncan MacKay, Jim Kennedy, Bobby Evans and Bertie Peacock were all in regular attendance.

Steve Chalmers and Neil Mochan were joint top scorers with a dozen goals each. Four of Mochan's goals were from the penalty spot, and he also scored all five, one of which was a penalty, when Celtic beat St Mirren in a Cup replay. John Divers scored a hat-trick from the inside-left position when Dunfermline were beaten 4–2 in November, but there was otherwise little to write home about on the goalscoring front.

The Bhoys finished the season with a scoring flourish, netting eight times in the last two games. Airdrie were beaten 5–2 (with a hat-trick from Chalmers), but St Mirren held Celtic to a 3–3 draw at Parkhead (two goals from Chalmers and one from Mochan). It had been a far from satisfactory season. They had scored 73 goals in the 34 games played but had only won 12, lost 13 and drawn nine. Their ninth position in the table was the joint second lowest since they had entered the Scottish League in 1890.

1959-60 LEAGUE RECORD

Opponents	Home	Away
Aberdeen	1-1	2-3
Airdrieonians	0-0	5-2
Arbroath	4-0	5-0
Ayr United	2-3	1-1
Clyde	1-1	3-3
Dundee	2-3	0-2
Dunfermline Athletic	4-2	2-3
Hearts	3-4	1-3
Hibernian	1-0	3-3
Kilmarnock	2-0	1-2
Motherwell	5-1	2-1
Partick Thistle	2-4	1-3
Raith Rovers	1-0	3-0
Rangers	0-1	1-3
St Mirren	3-3	3-0
Stirling Albion	1-1	2-2
Third Lanark	4-0	2-4

A-Z OF CELTIC

The Parkhead anthology,
presented alphabetically

A is for Auld. Midfield genius Bertie Auld is often credited, along with Jock Stein of course, for starting the great Celtic revival of the mid-1960s.

B is for Basle, who were beaten 10-1 on aggregate in the European Cup-Winner's Cup in September/October 1963. Celtic went on to reach the Semi-Finals that year.

C is for Cup victories. Celtic have won the Scottish Cup on 30 occasions, the first being in 1892 and the latest in 1995.

D is for Doubles. Celtic have completed the League and Scottish Cup Double on 11 occasions.

E is for Europe, and in particular for the European Cup triumph of 1967 when Inter Milan were beaten 2-1 in the Final – and Celtic also won all three domestic trophies.

F is for Five. Celtic scored five times in each of their first two recognised League matches, beating Hearts 5-0 and Cambuslang 5-2, both games being played in August 1890.

G is for a Goal a Game. Jimmy McGrory scored 398 goals in 378 League games, an average of just over a goal per game.

H is for Helenio Herrera, the Inter manager who said after the European Cup final: 'We can have no complaints. Celtic deserved their victory… Although we lost, the match was a victory for sport.'

I is for Interlude – the years of World War II, when Celtic signed virtually no guest players and seemed to take little interest in the wartime competitions.

J is for the Jungle – that part of the ground now gone forever.

K is for Kevin Kelly, the Celtic chairman who, at a time of great crisis for the club, proposed a move to a new stadium at Cambuslang. He was eventually forced to relinquish the chairmanship in favour of Fergus McCann.

L is for League Championship and League Cup wins. Celtic have won the League Championship 35 times, and have carried off the League Cup on 10 occasions.

M is for McCann – Fergus of that ilk, who took over from Kevin Kelly and promised so much.

N is for the new North Stand, opened in August 1995 with its green and white tape duly cut by adopted Scot Rod Stewart.

O is for Old Firm – the tremendous rivalry between the great Glasgow clubs, which has gone on for more than a hundred years.

P is for Paradise…need one say more?

Q is for Quinn – Jimmy Quinn, a rampaging tiger of a centre-forward who scored 216 times in his 331 Celtic appearances.

R is for Raith Rovers who, it must be admitted, humbled the mighty Celtic when they won the 1994 Coca-Cola Cup Final on penalties. Poor Paul McStay…

S is for Stein – a living legend until his untimely demise in September 1985.

T is for the Thomson Tragedy. John Thomson was one of Celtic's finest ever goalkeepers. He died following an accidental injury in an Old Firm game in September 1931.

U is for Unhappy Times – there have not really been many, all things considered, but the period of disruption and mounting debt during the early 1990s was one of them.

V is for Vale of Leven, beaten 9-1 in Celtic's first ever League season. This victory was all the more remarkable because Celtic had previously lost the away fixture 3-1.

W is for Brother Walfrid, widely regarded as the founder of Celtic Football Club.

X is for Neuchatel Xamax, the Swiss team who beat Celtic 5-2 on aggregate in the 1991-92 UEFA Cup. All right, it was not the most inspiring result – but you try finding a suitable X!

Y is for Sunny Jim Young, another of Celtic's great players who made almost 450 appearances between 1903 and 1917.

Z is for Zero – Packy Bonner's favourite number! The magic figure appeared against the name of the opposition on 250 occasions while Packy was in goal.

THROUGH THE YEARS
SEPTEMBER

1890
September
6

Celtic played Rangers in the Scottish Cup for the first time. They were to go out to Dumbarton at the Quarter-Final stage, but for now the important thing was that they beat the gentlemen of Ibrox by a Willie Groves goal.

1931
September
5

Tragedy occurred at an Old Firm meeting at Ibrox when an accidental collision led to the death of goalkeeper John Thomson. Left without defensive cover, Thomson dived bravely at the feet of Rangers' Sam English and was kicked in the head. He suffered a depressed fracture of the skull and died in hospital later that evening.

1938
September
10

In the last pre-war season Rangers were beaten 6-2 at Parkhead, Malky MacDonald scoring a hat-trick. A week earlier, Hearts had been beaten 5-1 in Edinburgh and, on 24 September, Raith Rovers were beaten 6-1.

1946

September

Celtic failed to win a September game in the first postwar season. They lost their three League games, which included defeats at Parkhead by Third Lanark (4-1) and Rangers (3-2), and also lost a League Cup game 4-2 at Hibernian. They did, however, manage a 0-0 draw at home to Third Lanark in the League Cup on 28 September.

1961

September

5

Bobby Lennox signed for Celtic. It was to be some time before he was to be given the nickname of a citrus fruit, an appendage which stuck after a newspaper reported the Celtic scorer as 'Lemon'.

1985

September

10

Celtic's greatest manager, Jock Stein, died in Cardiff, having suffered a heart attack following an International at Ninian Park. He was a few weeks short of his 63rd birthday.

BOGEY TEAMS

In the early days there were no bogey teams as far as mighty Celtic were concerned – though there were a few slip-ups.

Kilmarnock beat the Bhoys occasionally and in 1922-23 did the double over them, winning 2-1 at Parkhead and 4-3 at their own place. Of course Rangers obtained a victory from time to time, while Motherwell had something of a purple patch in the late 1920s, beating the Celts 2-1 and 3-1 in 1927-28, and 2-1 and 4-0 (at Parkhead) in 1929-30.

After the Second World War, Celtic had to endure a somewhat barren period. With their fortunes at a low ebb, it was inevitable that some teams would prosper at their expense, and it tended to be Aberdeen and, perhaps rather surprisingly, Third Lanark who came off best. Aberdeen had done the double over Celtic in the last pre-war season and they won the first three League encounters after the war. In 1946-47 they won 6-2 at Pittodrie, and later compounded the felony by winning 5-1 at Parkhead. Aberdeen finished in third place in the League that season, while Celtic finished seventh. Over the next six seasons, Aberdeen won six more League encounters, drew one and lost five. They also beat Celtic 1-0 in a Scottish Cup game in 1949-50.

Third Lanark did even better between seasons 1946-47 and 1951-52. During this period they notched up seven wins and four draws, losing on only one occasion. In the first of these seasons they won 4-1 at Parkhead, while in 1947-48 they won 5-1 at home and 3-1 in Paradise. Third Lanark then proceded to do the double for the second year running, winning 3-2 at home and 2-1 at Parkhead. Celtic gained their first postwar League win over them in 1949-50. The Celts won 2-1 at home, but went down 1-0 away.

Third Lanark's record was all the more remarkable because their overall League performance at the time was not all that spectacular. During this period they never finished higher than seventh in the table and in 1950-51, when they drew at Parkhead and won at home, they finished 13th out of the 16 teams then in the Scottish First Division. Celtic finished seventh.

Rangers were having a much better time of it. Between 1946-47 and 1952-53 they won the First Division Championship four times, and finished as runners-up at the end of the remaining three seasons. Celtic lost to them nine times, drew three times and won twice. The Celts suffered three 4-0 defeats − one at home and two at Ibrox. Things changed after that, and Celtic won the Championship in 1953-54, but they did not complete a League double over Rangers until 1971-72.

Since the mid-1950s, no team has consistently achieved spectacular success against Celtic. Motherwell won at Parkhead in 1974-75, and again in 1975-76, while in 1985-86 Celtic failed to win any of their four League encounters with Dundee United. They still won the Championship, however, with United coming third in the table. In 1996-97 Celtic lost all four against Rangers.

Bogey teams are similarly hard to find in the cup competitions, but Celtic were knocked out of the Scottish Cup by Kilmarnock in 1924, the 1929 Semi-Final, 1938, the 1957 Semi-Final replay, and in 1978. Motherwell did the same in 1932, 1939, 1976, the 1991 Semi-Final and in 1994.

LEAGUE RECORD

The Cups may have the glamour – but League success has always been uppermost in Parkhead minds.

Season	Division	P	W	D	L	F-A	Pts	Pos
1890-91	One	18	11	3	4	48-21	21★	3rd
1891-92	One	22	16	3	3	62-21	35	2nd
1892-93	One	18	14	1	3	54-25	29	1st
★ Division One Champions ★								
1893-94	One	18	14	1	3	53-32	29	1st
★ Division One Champions ★								
1894-95	One	18	11	4	3	50-29	26	2nd
1895-96	One	18	15	—	3	64-25	30	1st
★ Division One Champions ★								
1896-97	One	18	10	4	4	42-18	24	4th
1897-98	One	18	15	3	—	56-13	33	1st
★ Division One Champions ★								
1898-99	One	18	11	2	5	51-33	24	3rd
1899-1900	One	18	9	7	2	46-27	25	2nd
1900-01	One	20	13	3	4	49-28	29	2nd
1901-02	One	18	11	4	3	38-28	26	2nd
1902-03	One	22	8	10	4	36-30	26	5th
1903-04	One	26	18	2	6	69-28	38	3rd
1904-05	One	26	18	5	3	68-31	41	1st
★ Division One Champions ★								

Season	Division	P	W	D	L	F-A	Pts	Pos
1905-06	One	30	24	1	5	76-19	49	1st
★	Division One Champions						★	
1906-07	One	34	23	9	2	80-30	55	1st
★	Division One Champions						★	
1907-08	One	34	24	7	3	86-27	55	1st
★	Division One Champions						★	
1908-09	One	34	23	5	6	71-24	51	1st
★	Division One Champions						★	
1909-10	One	34	24	6	4	63-22	54	1st
★	Division One Champions						★	
1910-11	One	34	15	11	8	48-18	41	5th
1911-12	One	34	17	11	6	58-33	45	2nd
1912-13	One	34	22	5	7	53-28	49	2nd
1913-14	One	38	30	5	3	81-14	65	1st
★	Division One Champions						★	
1914-15	One	38	30	5	3	91-25	65	1st
★	Division One Champions						★	
1915-16	One	38	32	3	3	116-23	67	1st
★	Division One Champions						★	
1916-17	One	38	27	10	1	79-17	64	1st
★	Division One Champions						★	
1917-18	One	34	24	7	3	66-26	55	2nd
1918-19	One	34	26	6	2	71-22	58	1st
★	Division One Champions						★	

Season	Division	P	W	D	L	F-A	Pts	Pos
1919–20	One	42	29	10	3	89-31	68	2nd
1920–21	One	42	30	6	6	86-35	66	2nd
1921–22	One	42	27	13	2	83-20	67	1st
★ Division One Champions ★								
1922–23	One	38	19	8	11	52-39	46	3rd
1923–24	One	38	17	12	9	56-33	46	3rd
1924–25	One	38	18	8	12	77-44	44	4th
1925–26	One	38	25	8	5	97-40	58	1st
★ Division One Champions ★								
1926–27	One	38	21	7	10	101-55	49	3rd
1927–28	One	38	23	9	6	93-39	55	2nd
1928–29	One	38	22	7	9	67-44	51	2nd
1929–30	One	38	22	5	11	88-46	49	4th
1930–31	One	38	24	10	4	101-34	58	2nd
1931–32	One	38	20	8	10	94-50	48	3rd
1932–33	One	38	20	8	10	75-44	48	4th
1933–34	One	38	18	11	9	78-53	47	3rd
1934–35	One	38	24	4	10	92-45	52	2nd
1935–36	One	38	32	2	4	115-33	66	1st
★ Division One Champions ★								
1936–37	One	38	22	8	8	89-58	52	3rd
1937–38	One	38	27	7	4	114-42	61	1st
★ Division One Champions ★								
1938–39	One	38	20	8	10	99-53	48	2nd
1946–47	A	30	13	6	11	53-55	32	7th
1947–48	A	30	10	5	15	41-56	25	12th
1948–49	A	30	12	7	11	48-40	31	6th
1949–50	A	30	14	7	9	51-50	35	5th
1950–51	A	30	12	5	13	48-46	29	7th
1951–52	A	30	10	8	12	52-55	28	9th

Season	Division	P	W	D	L	F-A	Pts	Pos
1952–53	A	30	11	7	12	51-54	29	8th
1953–54	A	30	20	3	7	72-29	43	1st
★	Division A Champions						★	
1954–55	A	30	19	8	3	76-37	46	2nd
1955–56	A	34	16	9	9	55-39	41	5th
1956–57	One	34	15	8	11	58-43	38	5th
1957–58	One	34	19	8	7	84-47	46	3rd
1958–59	One	34	14	8	12	70-53	36	6th
1959–60	One	34	12	9	13	73-59	33	9th
1960–61	One	34	15	9	10	64-46	39	4th
1961–62	One	34	19	8	7	81-37	46	3rd
1962–63	One	34	19	6	9	76-44	44	4th
1963–64	One	34	19	9	6	89-34	47	3rd
1964–65	One	34	16	5	13	76-57	37	8th
1965–66	One	34	27	3	4	106-30	57	1st
★	Division One Champions						★	
1966–67	One	34	26	6	2	111-33	58	1st
★	Division One Champions						★	
1967–68	One	34	30	3	1	106-24	63	1st
★	Division One Champions						★	
1968–69	One	34	23	8	3	89-32	54	1st
★	Division One Champions						★	
1969–70	One	34	27	3	4	96-33	57	1st
★	Division One Champions						★	
1970–71	One	34	25	6	3	89-23	56	1st
★	Division One Champions						★	

Season	Division	P	W	D	L	F-A	Pts	Pos
1971-72	One	34	28	4	2	96-28	60	1st
⭐ Division One Champions ⭐								
1972-73	One	34	26	5	3	93-28	57	1st
⭐ Division One Champions ⭐								
1973-74	One	34	23	7	4	82-27	53	1st
⭐ Division One Champions ⭐								
1974-75	One	34	20	5	9	81-41	45	3rd
1975-76	Premier	36	21	6	9	71-42	48	2nd
1976-77	Premier	36	23	9	4	79-39	55	1st
⭐ Premier Division Champions ⭐								
1977-78	Premier	36	15	6	15	63-54	36	5th
1978-79	Premier	36	21	6	9	61-37	48	1st
⭐ Premier Division Champions ⭐								
1979-80	Premier	36	18	11	7	61-38	47	2nd
1980-81	Premier	36	26	4	6	84-37	56	1st
⭐ Premier Division Champions ⭐								
1981-82	Premier	36	24	7	5	79-33	55	1st
⭐ Premier Division Champions ⭐								
1982-83	Premier	36	25	5	6	90-36	55	2nd
1983-84	Premier	36	21	8	7	80-41	50	2nd
1984-85	Premier	36	22	8	6	77-30	52	2nd
1985-86	Premier	36	20	10	6	67-38	50	1st
⭐ Premier Division Champions ⭐								
1986-87	Premier	44	27	9	8	90-41	63	2nd

Season	Division	P	W	D	L	F-A	Pts	Pos
1987-88	Premier	44	31	10	3	79-23	72	1st

⭐ **Premier Division Champions** ⭐

Season	Division	P	W	D	L	F-A	Pts	Pos
1988-89	Premier	36	21	4	11	66-44	46	3rd
1989-90	Premier	36	10	14	12	37-37	34	5th
1990-91	Premier	36	17	7	12	52-38	41	3rd
1991-92	Premier	44	26	10	8	88-42	62	3rd
1992-93	Premier	44	24	12	8	68-41	60	3rd
1993-94	Premier	44	15	20	9	51-38	50	4th
1994-95	Premier	36	11	18	7	39-33	51	4th
1995-96	Premier	36	24	11	1	74-25	83	2nd
1996-97	Premier	36	23	6	7	78-32	75	2nd

⋆ *Celtic were deducted four points for infringements*

THROUGH THE YEARS
OCTOBER

1895
October
26

Celtic recorded their record League win, 11-0 over Dundee. Willie Ferguson scored five of the goals.

1911
October
25

Patsy Gallagher signed for Celtic. The Mighty Atom, as he was sometimes known, was to play a major part in the club's continuing success story.

1937
October
16

At the age of 33, Jimmy McGrory played his last game. Celtic beat Queen's Park 4-3, and of course McGrory scored.

1956
October
31

Celtic won the League Cup for the first time, when they beat Partick Thistle 3-0 in a replay.

1957
October
19

Championship winners Rangers were favourites to lift the League Cup. In the event they did not quite make it, as Celtic were rampant – and more than eager to retain the trophy. The Celts held a comfortable 2-0 lead at half-time but really went for it in the second period. They were already 6-1 up when they were awarded a penalty in the 90th minute, and so completed a record scoreline for a League Cup Final. The scorers were John McPhail (3), Neil Mochan (2), Sammy Wilson and Willie Fernie (pen).

1969
October
25

This was the year in which Celtic won the League Cup twice. They won it for the fifth successive season when they beat St Johnstone 1-0, but they had also won it the previous April when they had beaten Hibs 6-2 in a Final delayed by damage caused by a fire at Hampden Park.

KEEPERS KORNER

The Celts have been blessed with several great last lines of defence. We look at a quintet of classic keepers.

 # DAVIE ADAMS

Big Davie Adams was one of Celtic's great keepers of the early days. Taking over from the formidable Dan McArthur (1892-1903), he made his Scottish League debut in a 1-0 victory over Hibernian on 26 September 1903, following an excellent display against Middlesbrough during a pre-season tour. He did well against Hibs, too, and he was to remain the number one choice for the next eight seasons.

A large man – he weighed in at 14 stone but was only just six feet tall – Adams was born in Oathlaw on 14 May 1883. He almost joined Falkirk as a junior, but manager Willie Maley took him on tour to Ireland with Celtic and signed him up while the team was staying in Dublin. It proved to be a wise decision, as Adams was later to help himself to six consecutive League Championship medals between 1904-05 and 1909-10, as well as another four 'gongs' for winning the Scottish Cup in 1904, 1907, 1908 and 1911. He also took part in the 'Hampden Riot' Final in 1909 when Celtic and Rangers drew 1-1 in the replay and the Cup was witheld.

Adams was the first keeper to abandon the green and white

and put on a jersey of a different colour. Ill-health dogged his career, but few would have noticed at the time. During his years at Celtic he was known to suffer from rheumatism, and also had to endure a number of attacks of pneumonia, but in the end he was forced to retire at the age of 29 due to problems with his eyes. He made 291 appearances for Celtic and kept clean sheets on 124 occasions. Davie Adams died in Edinburgh on 29 November 1948.

DAVIE ADAMS CELTIC APPS 1902-12				
League	FA Cup	League Cup	Europe	Total
248	43	—	—	291

 # CHARLIE SHAW

Wee Charlie Shaw was that rare phenomenon – a short but outstanding goalkeeper. Born in Twechar on 21 September 1885, he played English football with QPR, making 223 appearances for the London club, before joining Celtic in May 1913. Described as a 'wondrous little footballer', he soon established himself as a firm favourite with the fans. Playing right through the Great War, he missed not a single League game between August 1913 and September 1918 – a run of 193 consecutive matches.

During Shaw's first League season he had a run of ten consecutive clean sheets, and he conceded just 14 goals in a campaign of 38 matches. His subsequent seasons were almost as barren as far as the opposition was concerned, with 25 conceded in 1914-15, 23 in 1915-16, 17 in 1916-17, 24 in 1917-18 and 22 in 1918-19. Celtic started to leak a few more goals after the war – especially when Rangers began to get into their stride – but matters would have been worse had five foot six inch Charlie Shaw not been between the posts.

Shaw won Championship medals in 1913-14, 1914-15,

1915-16, 1916-17, 1918-19 and 1921-22 and he also won
Scottish Cup medals in 1914 and 1923. He had an extremely
loud voice and a remarkably commanding presence for one so
small and, in September 1916, he was rightly appointed club
captain. He played his last game for Celtic in January 1925, by
which time he had 436 games to his credit (a total not to be
equalled until Packy Bonner came on the scene) and had
prevented his opponents from scoring in 240 of them. Charlie
Shaw died in New York on 27 March 1938.

CHARLIE SHAW CELTIC APPS 1913-25				
League	FA Cup	League Cup	Europe	Total
420	16	—	—	436

JOE KENNAWAY

Born in Montreal on 25 January 1905, Joe Kennaway
played for Fall River against Celtic during the US tour
of 1931. John Thomson was the Celts' regular keeper at
the time but he was to die tragically following a goalless draw
at Ibrox in September of that year. So it was that, a few
months after making a significant impression on Willie Maley
in the Fall River game, Kennaway was on his way to Glasgow
and was soon making his Celtic debut in a 2-2 draw at
Motherwell.

The new keeper was injured in this first game – but, once
recovered, he went on to a great career, playing in every
League and Cup fixture in season 1934-35 and conceding an
average of a little over a goal per game during that campaign.
In the following season he conceded an average of rather less
than a goal per game. Celtic twice won the League title
(1935-36 and 1937-38) and the Cup (1933 and 1937) while
Kennaway was their principal custodian, his outstanding shot-
stopping being the main reason his side won the latter trophy

in 1933 when Motherwell went down 1-0 in the Final and Kennaway was hailed as the saviour of the day.

Joe Kennaway made 295 appearances and kept 83 clean sheets. He saved more penalties than almost any other Celtic goalkeeper – on one famous occasion felling Davie Meiklejohn of Rangers with a straight right, then saving the resultant spot-kick. His playing career ended with the outbreak of war and he died in Canada on 7 March 1969 at the age of 64.

JOE KENNAWAY CELTIC APPS 1931-39				
League	FA Cup	League Cup	Europe	Total
263	32	—	—	295

 # RONNIE SIMPSON

Nine years had elapsed since Ronnie Simpson last tasted glory, and a £4,000 move from Hibernian to Celtic in September 1964 was generally regarded as one last pay-day before the boots were hung up. But the superbly agile stopper was to cram in more awards over the next five years with Celtic than he could have dared imagine when making his debut for Queen's Park still 64 days shy of his 15th birthday.

Moving to Newcastle United following National Service in 1951, he enjoyed a nine-year stay in the English First Division, a stint highlighted by two FA Cup winner's medals, against Arsenal in 1952 and Manchester City three years later, before returning north to Easter Road in October 1960. Simpson's positional sense was immaculate and, despite his relative lack of inches for a keeper, he had little trouble cutting out the most accurate crosses from either wing.

Known as 'Faither' to his younger team-mates, Ronnie played 188 times for Celtic following his debut in November

1964, keeping a remarkable 91 clean sheets – almost one every two games – while amassing four Championship, one Scottish Cup and three League Cup medals.

Capped for the first time in April 1967 in a 3-2 European Championship victory over World Champions England, a further four were to follow, and Simpson was named Scottish Player of the Year a month later before crowning his glittering career with a European Cup winner's medal as part of the famous Lisbon Lions.

A shoulder injury forced Simpson to quit the game in 1970, but he made one last bow when, with the League title already won for the sixth successive year, Jock Stein decided to parade the Lions of Lisbon one last time, against Clyde in May 1971.

RONNIE SIMPSON CELTIC APPS 1964-70				
League	FA Cup	League Cup	Europe	Total
118	17	29	24	188

 # PACKY BONNER

Irish ace Patrick (Packy) Bonner was born in Co Donegal on 24 May 1960, and has to rank as one of the club's best keepers ever. Signed in 1978 by Jock Stein, a man not normally noted for his ability to pick good goalkeepers, he made his League debut in March 1979.

Bonner suffered some initial back problems but, by the start of the 1980–81 campaign, he was fully fit and able to replace Peter Latchford between the posts. He was ever-present in the League throughout 1980–81, 1981–82 and 1982–83.

Thereafter, he continued as Celtic's principal goalkeeper, allowing Latchford only the very occasional opportunity to show what he could do, until November 1991, when the excellent form of understudy Gordon Marshall led to Bonner being sidelined for a while.

Bonner's record, despite some strange lapses during the later stages of his career, had been a remarkable one, but in May 1994 – and to the horror and amazement of the Celtic faithful – he was given a free transfer. He was still a regular in the Eire side, having done a great deal to enhance the reputation of the Republic as an international footballing nation, and in July of that year won his 77th international cap. Bonner was about to join Kilmarnock, but new manager Tommy Burns brought him back to Celtic in time for the start of the 1994-95 season at Hampden Park.

Bonner earned an array of winners' medals: Premier Division Championship 1980-81, 1981-82, 1985-86, 1987-88, Scottish Cup 1985, 1989, 1995, and Scottish League Cup 1982-83.

In all, Packy Bonner made 632 appearances for Celtic, and kept more than 250 clean sheets – a truly remarkable record.

PACKY BONNER CELTIC APPS 1978-95				
League	FA Cup	League Cup	Europe	Total
483	54	60	35	632

BEST SEASON 3

Celtic had won everything in 1966–67 and might have been expected to ease up a bit during the following year.

To an extent they did – even going so far as to relinquish the Scottish Cup at the first hurdle, going down 2-0 at home to Dunfermline – but 1967-68 was nevertheless to prove an excellent League season.

It began with a comfortable 3-0 victory over Clyde, but this was followed by a 1-0 defeat at Ibrox. It was to end up being very much an Old Firm season with Rangers, as well as Celtic, losing only one game in the whole campaign. After a late-September 1-1 draw at home to St Johnstone, the Celts notched up eight wins on the trot, scoring 27 goals and conceding only three. They then played out another 1-1 draw, this time at home to Dundee United, before winning the next five.

With Ronnie Simpson the custodian for all but one game, Celtic conceded just 24 goals in 34 League encounters. Simpson, who kept clean sheets in almost half of all his Celtic games, kept the ball out of the net on 18 occasions. With Jim Craig at right-back, Tommy Gemmell at left-back and Billy McNeill ever-present at centre-half, Simpson had some very good cover. Bobby Murdoch and John Clark also played in most games, so the goals against tally was hardly surprising.

A lot of goals came from men wearing 8. Bobby Lennox twice scored four in a match while wearing the Number 8 shirt, while Steve Chalmers scored two on three occasions. Willie Wallace, sometimes wearing 8 and sometimes 9, scored a total of 21 League goals, while John Hughes scored seven, Billy McNeill six, Bobby Murdoch and Jimmy Johnstone five apiece and Bertie Auld four. Joe McBride also scored four, three of them coming in a game at Morton.

Having drawn with St Johnstone early in the season, Celtic beat them 6-1 in Perth. They also won 6-0 at Kilmarnock and scored five on five more occasions – one of which resulted in an unusual 5-4 scoreline at Dundee.

Celtic finished the campaign having won 30 of their 34 games, their one defeat being that early-season game at Ibrox. It was a magnificent record – and the Celts had also won the League Cup. Remarkably, they had beaten Dundee 5-3 in the Final of that competition, which meant that, by the season's end, they had put five past the team from Dens Park on three separate occasions.

1967-68 LEAGUE RECORD		
Opponents	**Home**	**Away**
Aberdeen	4-1	1-0
Airdrieonians	4-0	2-0
Clyde	3-0	3-2
Dundee	5-2	5-4
Dundee United	1-1	5-0
Dunfermline Athletic	3-2	2-1
Falkirk	3-0	3-0
Hearts	3-1	2-0
Hibernian	4-0	2-0
Kilmarnock	3-0	6-0
Morton	2-1	4-0
Motherwell	4-2	1-0
Partick Thistle	4-1	5-1
Raith Rovers	5-0	2-0
Rangers	2-2	0-1
St Johnstone	1-1	6-1
Stirling Albion	2-0	4-0

THROUGH THE YEARS
NOVEMBER

1887
November
6

A meeting was called at the parish hall of St Mary's to discuss the possibilty of forming a new football club. Brother Walfrid suggested it should be called Celtic.

1937
November
15

Willie Buchan, who had played 134 times for Celtic and scored 59 goals, was transferred to Blackpool for a fee of £10,000. He returned on loan during the war, but made just one further appearance in a Celtic shirt.

1961
November
8

Jimmy Johnstone signed for Celtic. He did not make his first team debut until March 1963, and was doubtless not very impressed with his team-mates. Celtic lost 6–0 at Kilmarnock.

1969
November
12

In the European Cup, Celtic defeated Benfica 3-0. Two weeks later they lost the second leg by the same score, and the decision as to which side went through to the Quarter-Final was left to Lady Luck. The Dutch referee produced a two and a half guilder piece and it fell to Billy McNeill to call. To McNeill's relief he made the right decision, and Celtic were through.

1983
November
2

Having lost the first leg 2-0, Celtic beat Sporting Lisbon 5-0 in the return UEFA Cup game.

1997
November
30

Celtic won the League Cup for the first time since 1982-83, when they beat Dundee United 3-0 in the Final and lifted the Coca-Cola trophy.

GREAT DEFENDERS

They say attack is the best form of defence – but you'll never win titles without keeping your back door shut tight! Here are some of the greatest Celtic defenders.

PETER WILSON

Peter Wilson was a right-half who made 395 appearances in the green and white between 1924 and 1934. Born in Beith on 26 March 1905, he played for Beith Amateurs before signing for Celtic in May 1923.

At first he jostled for the Number 4 shirt with Jimmy McStay, but he soon made it his own and was ever-present in season 1925–26, when he won a Championship medal and finished on the losing side in the Scottish Cup Final.

'Peter Wilson didn't pass the ball, he stroked it', wrote a sports journalist at the time, and these words accurately describe the Wilson style. He was ever cool in a crisis and had an immaculate footballing brain. He seldom seemed to hurry and the accuracy of his passes became almost legendary. He played four times for Scotland and won Cup winner's medals with Celtic in 1925, 1927, 1931 and 1933. He maintained his connection with football long after his playing days were over, becoming Kilmarnock's coach in 1953. Peter Wilson died in his home town of Beith on 13 February 1983.

PETER WILSON CELTIC RECORD 1923-34									
League		FA Cup		League Cup		Europe		Total	
Apps	Goals	Apps	Goals	Apps	Goals	Apps	Goals	Apps	Goals
344	14	51	1	—	—	—	—	395	15

BERTIE PEACOCK

Left-half Bertie Peacock was born in Coleraine on 29 September 1928. He played for Coleraine and Glentoran, where he scored the only goal of the 1949 Irish Cup Final against Derry City, before signing for Celtic in May 1948.

Playing initially as an inside-left, Peacock made his League debut in a 1-1 at Raith Rovers in January 1950, and his through balls were soon described as every bit as good as Pat McAuley's – high praise indeed. He established himself in the side in the 1950-51 season and, still at inside-left, scored nine League and Cup goals in an ever-present campaign.

During 1951-52 and 1952-53 he sometimes appeared in a Number 11 shirt and in October 1952 he scored both goals in a 2-1 win at Clyde. Peacock converted to left-half early in the 1953-54 campaign and was Celtic's regular Number 6 for the next eight years.

As a member of the great half-back line of Evans, Stein and Peacock, Bertie enjoyed tremendous success. The trio helped Celtic to win the Double in 1953-54 while, in October 1956, Peacock and Evans were both in the side which beat Partick Thistle 3-0, in a replayed Final which secured the League Cup for Celtic for the first time.

These were exciting times for the club and for Bertie Peacock, but there was to be a great deal more excitement a year later. Peacock was now the skipper and had the rather pleasant duty of lifting the League Cup high once more – this time after an incredible 7-1 thrashing of the club from Ibrox. The Celts were really rather pleased, and who could blame them?

Peacock played his part in the excellent Irish performance in the 1958 World Cup, where Swedish journalists called him the 'little black ant'. He made 30 Northern Ireland appearances while with Celtic, his last game at Parkhead being in the Scottish Cup, at home to Hibs in March 1961. He had made 453 appearances, and scored on 50 occasions.

BERTIE PEACOCK CELTIC RECORD 1949-61									
League		**FA Cup**		**League Cup**		**Europe**		**Total**	
Apps	**Goals**	**Apps**	**Goals**	**Apps**	**Goals**	**Apps**	**Goals**	**Apps**	**Goals**
318	33	56	7	79	10	—	—	453	50

 # BILLY McNEILL

Billy McNeill was the best centre-half Celtic ever had. Born in Bellshill on 2 March 1940, he signed for Celtic in August 1957 and made his debut in a 2-0 home win over Clyde in the League Cup on 23 August 1958. He proceeded to establish himself in the side and was so successful that he replaced Dunky MacKay as club captain at the start of the 1963-64 season.

Celtic had been going through a lean time on the trophy front and McNeill, hungry for success, considered a transfer to Tottenham during the summer of 1964. He finally decided to stay at Parkhead, and it proved a wise choice because, when Jock Stein took over in 1965, the Celts' fortunes took a decided turn for the better.

In April 1965 McNeill scored one of his trademark headed goals in the Scottish Cup Final to secure a 3-2 win over Dunfermline, and Celtic were back on the winning trail. Big

Billy was a giant at the heart of the defence, manager Stein calling him 'One of the greatest Celts of all time, an inspiring captain and a model for any young footballer'.

Over the years, Billy McNeill was to win nine League Championship medals, seven Scottish Cup and six League Cup winner's medals. Enough medals for the broadest of chests, you might have thought...but, of course, the big one came in May 1967 when the Celtic captain raised aloft the European Cup in Lisbon. Inter Milan had been beaten 2-1 in the Final and the Celtic defence had conceded only four more goals along the way.

Billy McNeill made 790 appearances in League, Cup and European competitions, as well as playing 29 times for Scotland. He led what was almost certainly the greatest of all the Celtic teams and, for good measure, scored 34 Celtic goals. He was a truly great player.

BILLY McNEILL CELTIC RECORD 1958-75									
League		FA Cup		League Cup		Europe		Total	
Apps	Goals	Apps	Goals	Apps	Goals	Apps	Goals	Apps	Goals
486	22	94	7	138	2	72	3	790	34

 # DANNY McGRAIN

Right-back Danny McGrain was born in Finnieston on 1 May 1950. Whisper it softly, but in his early days he was a confirmed supporter of Rangers. This little-known fact, however, did not stop him from signing on at Parkhead in May 1967.

McGrain created a very favourable impression at Celtic, making his debut as a substitute in a 2-2 draw at Dundee United in the League Cup during August 1970. He was to develop a tremendous understanding with Kenny Dalglish and prove himself to be a beautifully balanced player, as well as a sturdy full-back able to turn defence into attack as the occasion demanded – although goalscoring was not a strong point.

Like any footballer, McGrain had his ups and downs. He suffered a number of injuries and guided his team through some tough times as well as some very happy ones. When he led the side on a tour of Australia, he was proclaimed locally as the best footballer ever seen on that continent and was later described as 'the one world–class player left in Scotland'.

McGrain won 62 Scottish caps – a record for a Celtic player until it was later overtaken by Paul McStay – and truly entered the Scottish hall of football fame. His awards included the Scotland Player of the Year in 1977, an MBE in 1983 and a Glasgow honour, a civic medal for services to sport, in September 1987. As club captain, he led Celtic to a number of triumphs and in all he won seven Championship medals, five Scottish Cup medals and was on the winning side in two League Cup Finals – the first being an unusual 6-3 victory over Hibernian.

Danny McGrain's playing career with the club he came to love saw him amass 603 League and Cup appearances, as well as representing Celtic in Europe on 54 occasions. He played a single season with Hamilton after leaving Parkhead.

DANNY McGRAIN CELTIC RECORD 1967-87									
League		FA Cup		League Cup		Europe		Total	
Apps	Goals	Apps	Goals	Apps	Goals	Apps	Goals	Apps	Goals
439	4	60	1	104	3	54	—	657	8

ALAN STUBBS

Six-foot, Merseyside-born central defender Alan Stubbs settled into the Glasgow scene with no apparent discomfort following his big-money transfer from Bolton Wanderers in the summer of 1996. He'd made his name not in the red of Liverpool or the blue of Everton but the white of Bolton Wanderers, where he'd been a trainee before turning full pro in 1990 and making his first-team debut in season 1990–91.

Along with fellow hopeful Jason McAteer he helped them into the 1995 Coca-Cola Cup Final and caught many a top club's eye. But while Eire international McAteer secured his future with a transfer to Liverpool, Stubbs remained to play 25 games in Bolton's brief Premiership stay. Celtic then made their move, and, though in and out of the side, he clocked up over 20 games in the hoops

Still only 23 at the time of his transfer, he'd already made more than 200 League appearances for the Trotters, giving him the benefit of experience as well as youth. He'd worked hard on his weakness, a tendency to dwell on the ball, and had secured an England B cap under Terry Venables who called him 'a fair player…but it's early days yet'. Whether future honours were to be won under Glenn Hoddle was of less interest to the green half of Glasgow than his ability to help Celtic to a much-needed Championship. But whole-hearted 'Stubbsie' will do his best.

ALAN STUBBS CELTIC RECORD 1996-(97)									
League		FA Cup		League Cup		Europe		Total	
Apps	Goals	Apps	Goals	Apps	Goals	Apps	Goals	Apps	Goals
20	—	4	—	1	—	1	—	26	—

THE WAR YEARS

During the First World War, English League football was suspended for the duration after the 1914–15 season.

Although the Scottish Cup was abandoned, the Scottish League carried on, even though there was inevitable disruption for the leading teams – and the players' wages were reduced to a maximum of £2 per week.

Football was thought to be good for morale and no doubt when Celtic supporters, up to their armpits in the mud of the trenches, learned that their side had won the Championship for the third successive season in 1917, morale did improve just a little. Those supporters dreamed of Paradise. Sadly, many were soon to find themselves there – as were some of their playing heroes who also failed to return from the front.

In the Second World War, things were rather different. The day after Celtic beat Clyde 1–0 at the start of what was to have been the 1939–40 Scottish League season, war was again declared – and this time all League football was suspended. Questions of morale were again raised and before long the government decreed that football was permissible, but it was clearly not possible to organise the game on national lines. Regional leagues were therefore organised across Britain.

During the first wartime season, Celtic played in the Regional League (Western) but then moved to the Southern League, where they remained until 1946. The Scottish Cup was suspended, as it had been in the First World War, but a Southern League Cup and a Scottish Summer Cup were both instituted. Celtic entered these competitions but, remarkably in view of the size, reputation and previous achievements of the club, failed to win any of them.

There were several reasons for this. A little over a year after the outbreak of war, Willie Maley finally resigned as secretary-manager, making way for Jimmy McStay. The latter soon found dissension in the ranks at Celtic and little enthusiasm on the board for wartime football. No doubt McStay would have liked to do as other managers were doing, and attract guest players to Parkhead. During this time Stanley Matthews turned out for both Rangers and Morton and Matt Busby played for Hibernian, but no one came to Celtic.

Naturally the club's resources were depleted due to the war. Joe Kennaway returned to America, Jock Morrison was working in the mines and Willie Lyon, George Paterson and Frank Murphy all joined the forces. Celtic sometimes found themselves in the wrong half of the table – in the first season they finished 13th in the Regional League (Western) – and for their supporters this was particularly galling, as Rangers seemed to be more or less always at the top.

Old Firm rivalry boiled over on several occasions. In September 1941 at Ibrox, bottles were thrown, Jimmy Delaney and Johnny Crum were sent off and a number of spectators were arrested. This led to the closure of Celtic Park for a month, a decision which understandably upset the faithful. Later, on New Year's Day 1943, Rangers beat Celtic 8-1 and Malcolm MacDonald and Matt Lynch were sent off for fighting each other, although this cannot perhaps strictly be attributed to traditional rivalry.

Towards the end of the war, Celtic's results began to improve. They finished second to Rangers at the end of both 1943-44 and 1944-45, although when Rangers won the Southern League (A Division) title in 1945-46, the Celts could only manage fourth position. It was, in fact, to be some time before the glory days would return to Celtic Park once more.

GAFFERSPEAK

We offer some words of wisdom that have emanated from the Parkhead manager's office over the years.

'They never die who live in the hearts of those they leave behind.'
Written on a memorial card by Willie Maley,
after the death of goalkeeper John Thomson

'It has been to me the end of my football career and has robbed me of the very tang of life. Football has been my thoughts morning, noon and night for all the 52 years I have been in it, and it has been very hard to drop out of my regular ways.'
Willie Maley after he had been forced
into retirement in 1940, at the age of 71

'No hint of a change had been given me when I prepared to leave for two weeks' holiday. I made up the groundsmen's wages just before I left and went down to Ayr with my family.'
Jimmy McStay, following his enforced resignation in 1945

'He has the football brain and positional sense of an Alec Thomson.'
Jimmy McGrory on Bobby Murdoch

'Speaking as a former centre-half, he's like having a brick wall behind you.'
Billy McNeill on Packy Bonner

'I only want you if you're willing to play one hundred percent for the jersey. If not, stay at Kilmarnock.'
Billy McNeill to Davie Provan

'He's a tremendous player. What a prospect he is for the future!'   *Billy McNeill on Derek Whyte.*

'Celtic appointed me when I was probably inexperienced, and sacked me when I was more capable of doing the job.'
David Hay

'I doubted if I had the right personality. I am rather reserved, at least in public. I didn't know if I had the knowledge, or the ability to spot players.'
Liam Brady, on his brief spell as Celtic manager

'I told him to stay off the play, to get his passes in rather than take players on. I told him to be selfish.'
Coach Frank Connor on Paul McStay in 1993

'My job is to leap Celtic ahead of Rangers. I'll certainly be my own harshest critic. If the team has made no significant progress I'll be off. I won't need directors to tell me to go.'
Lou Macari on his appointment as manager.
He was sacked eight months later.

'If I spend millions for a player I would want it to be an investment for this club, rather than someone who is going to be freed at the end of an expensive contract.'
Tommy Burns

'Tosh has natural ability and can put killer balls into the box, and we need that.'   *Tommy Burns on Tosh McKinlay*

'Kenny Dalglish will never make it in English football. He's too weak, and hasn't got the skill or temperament for our game.'
Terry Neill, 1977

THROUGH THE YEARS
DECEMBER

1887

December

Eager to start building a team, three of Celtic's founders – Brother Walfrid, John Glass and Pat Welsh – called at the home of one Tom Maley to persuade him to sign up. He was out, but his brother Willie, a half-back with Third Lanark, was in and so they persuaded him to join Celtic as well. So began Willie Maley's association with Celtic Football Club – an association that was to last for 53 years.

1888

December

8

During the first Scottish Cup campaign, Celtic beat Clyde 9–2. Tom Maley scored a hat-trick and Willie Groves netted four times.

1935

December

21

Jimmy McGrory broke the British League scoring record. He did it in style, scoring a hat-trick in a 5–3 win over Aberdeen.

1951
December
8

Jock Stein began his career as a Celtic player. He apparently made a quiet debut but, although far better-known for his later managerial achievements, he was to prove himself an accomplished centre-half. He played in 148 games.

1956
December
22

John Higgins scored four times as Celtic won 7-3 at Airdrie.

1969
December

Between 17 and 27 December, Celtic scored 18 League goals at Parkhead. They beat Dundee United 7-2, Kilmarnock 3-1 and Partick Thistle 8-1. John Hughes scored six of them.

THE KITBAG

Celtic's green and white hoops are famous the world over – and have been for something approaching a hundred years. But the team did not always play in hooped shirts.

In the very beginning Celtic wore white, but green stripes soon appeared and around the turn of the century the familiar hooped jerseys started to be worn on a regular basis.

Comparatively few football teams take the field in hoops – only Morton and, in England, Queens Park Rangers come instantly to mind – and this may be because the strip tends to make players appear somewhat more 'rotund' than they actually are. Perhaps it's just as well that Paul Gascoigne joined Rangers. In any event, Celtic were happy with their strip and it has remained largely unaltered ever since.

Of course it has sometimes been necessary to employ a change strip for away games, either because of a colour clash or because change strips provide opportunities for the marketing of additional replica kits. In Scotland, the wearing of green by Hibs has forced a change of strip on Celtic for visits to Easter Road, but for most domestic encounters such a change has been largely unnecessary. This has not stopped it happening, though. Any excuse will do, and Celtic have been known to wear all-white shirts with the club emblem, all-green shirts with the club emblem and, for a short while, shirts with green and black vertical stripes.

Supporters generally do not like change (away fans are

often heard to complain when an unlucky strip is worn) so it is good that the Bhoys have almost always trotted out at Parkhead suitably dressed, although there have been some minor alterations over the years. With the advent of European football in the early 1960s, the fact that numbers were not carried on shirts was beginning to cause problems. Nobody had bothered much before, because the entire population of Scotland knew who Billy McNeill, Bertie Peacock and Jim Kennedy were, but naturally the continentals were less well informed. Numbers on the players' shorts appeared insufficient.

Further confusion was caused in September 1973 when, for the first home game of the season, every Celtic player wore Number 8. This was to celebrate the fact that the side had won eight consecutive Scottish League Championships, and the Bhoys duly beat Clyde 5-0, the goals coming from Number 8 Lennox (3), Number 8 Dalglish and Number 8 McGrain. It seemed to work, as Celtic went on to win consecutive Championship number nine. Had they won it again for the next three years, presumably everyone would have ended up as substitutes…

As far as shirts are concerned, there has also been the odd change in recent times – most notably the reluctant addition of numbers. During the 1980s, the name of sponsors CR Smith began to adorn the chests of one and all and, to celebrate the club's centenary season, in 1987 a smart new outfit was commissioned. In truth, this looked little different from the previous version, except that the lucky four-leafed clover was replaced as Celtic's symbol by a Celtic cross which had been the original club crest.

As the world moves on, many things become altered. Fabrics have certainly altered since football's early days, but overall Celtic is to be congratulated for sticking to tradition and leaving the green and white pretty well untouched for almost a century.

EUROPEAN CUP

Winners at the first time of asking, Celtic have contested this major trophy 15 times.

Stage	Opponents	Home	Away	Agg
1966-67				
Round 1	Zurich	2-0	3-0	5-0
Round 2	Nantes	3-1	3-1	6-2
Quarter-Final	Vojvodina	2-0	0-1	2-1
Semi-Final	Dukla Prague	3-1	0-0	3-1
Final	Inter Milan	—	—	2-1
1967-68				
Round 1	Dynamo Kiev	1-2	1-1	2-3
1968-69				
Round 1	St Etienne	4-0	0-2	4-2
Round 2	Red Star Belgrade	5-1	1-1	6-2
Quarter-Final	AC Milan	0-1	0-0	0-1
1969-70				
Round 1	Basle	2-0	0-0	2-0
Round 2	Benfica	3-0	0-3	3-3
Celtic won on the toss of a coin				
Quarter-Final	Fiorentina	3-0	0-1	3-1
Semi-Final	Leeds United	2-1	1-0	3-1
Final	Feyenoord	—	—	1-2
1970-71				
Round 1	KPV Kokkola	9-0	5-0	14-0
Round 2	Waterford	3-2	7-0	10-2
Quarter-Final	Ajax	1-0	0-3	1-3

Stage	Opponents	Home	Away	Agg
1971-72				
Round 1	BK 1903 Copenhagen	3-0	1-2	4-2
Round 2	Sliema Wanderers	5-0	2-1	7-1
Quarter-Final	Ujpest Dozsa	1-1	2-1	3-2
Semi-Final	Inter Milan	0-0	0-0	0-0
Celtic lost on penalties				
1972-73				
Round 1	Rosenborg	2-1	3-1	5-2
Round 2	Ujpest Dozsa	2-1	0-3	2-4
1973-74				
Round 1	Turku	3-0	6-1	9-1
Round 2	Vejle	0-0	1-0	1-0
Quarter-Final	Basle	4-2	2-3	6-5
Semi-Final	Atletico Madrid	0-0	0-2	0-2
1974-75				
Round 1	Olympiakos Piraeus	1-1	0-2	1-3
1977-78				
Round 1	Jeunesse D'Esch	5-0	6-1	11-1
Round 2	SW Innsbruck	2-1	0-3	2-4
1979-80				
Round 1	Partizan Tirana	4-1	0-1	4-2
Round 2	Dundalk	3-2	0-0	3-2
Quarter-Final	Real Madrid	2-0	0-3	2-3
1981-82				
Round 1	Juventus	1-0	0-2	1-2
1982-83				
Round 1	Ajax Amsterdam	2-2	2-1	4-3
Round 2	Real Sociedad	2-1	0-2	2-3

Stage	Opponents	Home	Away	Agg
1986-87				
Round 1	Shamrock Rovers	2-0	1-0	3-0
Round 2	Dynamo Kiev	1-1	1-3	2-4
1988-89				
Round 1	Honved	4-0	0-1	4-1
Round 2	Werder Bremen	0-1	0-0	0-1

EUROPEAN CUP WINNERS' CUP

Though they've yet to reach the Final, Celtic have had eight attempts at ECWC glory.

Stage	Opponents	Home	Away	Agg
1963-64				
Round 1	Basle	5-0	5-1	10-1
Round 2	Dynamo Zagreb	3-0	1-2	4-2
Quarter-Final	Slovan Bratislava	1-0	1-0	2-0
Semi-Final	MTK Budapest	3-0	0-4	3-4
1965-66				
Round 1	Go Ahead Deventer	1-0	6-0	7-0
Round 2	Aarhus	2-0	1-0	3-0
Quarter-Final	Dynamo Kiev	3-0	1-1	4-1
Semi-Final	Liverpool	1-0	0-2	1-2
1975-76				
Round 1	Valur Reykjavik	7-0	2-0	9-0
Round 2	Boavista	3-1	0-0	3-1
Quarter-Final	Sachsenring Zwickau	1-1	0-1	1-2
1980-81				
Preliminary	Diosgyor	6-0	1-2	7-2
Round 1	Poli Timisoara	2-1	0-1	2-2

Celtic lost on away goals

Stage	Opponents	Home	Away	Agg
1984-85				
Round 1	Ghent	3-0	0-1	3-1
Round 2	Rapid Vienna	3-0	1-3	4-3

Celtic lost the replay 0-1 following a Rapid Vienna protest about crowd violence

Stage	Opponents	Home	Away	Agg
1985-86				
Round 1	Atletico Madrid	1-2	1-1	2-3

Stage	Opponents	Home	Away	Agg
1989-90				
Round 1	Partizan Belgrade	5-4	1-2	6-6

Celtic lost on away goals

Stage	Opponents	Home	Away	Agg
1995-96				
Round 1	Dinamo Batumi	4-0	3-2	7-2
Round 2	Paris St Germain	0-3	0-1	0-4

INTER-CITIES FAIRS/UEFA CUP

The first, and also the most recent European competition in which Celtic have participated.

Stage	Opponents	Home	Away	Agg
1962-63				
Round 1	Valencia	2-2	2-4	4-6
1964-65				
Round 1	Leixoes Sporting	3-0	1-1	4-1
Round 2	Barcelona	0-0	1-3	1-3
1976-77				
Round 1	Wisia Krakow	2-2	0-2	2-4
1983-84				
Round 1	Aarhus	1-0	4-1	5-1
Round 2	Sporting Lisbon	5-0	0-2	5-2
Round 3	Nottingham Forest	1-2	0-0	1-2
1987-88				
Round 1	Borussia Dortmund	2-1	0-2	2-3
1991-92				
Round 1	Ekeren	2-0	1-1	3-1
Round 2	Neuchatel Xamax	1-0	1-5	2-5

Stage	Opponents	Home	Away	Agg
1992-93				
Round 1	Cologne	3-0	0-2	3-2
Round 2	Borussia Dortmund	1-2	0-1	1-3
1993-94				
Round 1	Young Boys Berne	1-0	0-0	1-0
Round 2	Sporting Lisbon	1-0	0-2	1-2
1996-97				
Qualifier	Kosice	1-0	0-0	1-0
Round 1	Hamburg	0-2	0-2	0-4
1997-98				
Qualifier 1	Inter Cable-Tel	5-0	3-0	8-0
Qualifier 2	FC Tirol Innsbruck	6-3	1-2	7-5
Round 1	Liverpool	2-2	0-0	2-2

Celtic lost on away goals

Celtic's record against European opposition

Country	P	W	D	L	F-A
Albania	2	1	—	1	4-2
Austria	7	3	—	4	13-13
Belgium	4	2	1	1	6-2
Czechoslovakia	4	3	1	—	5-1
Denmark	8	6	1	1	13-3
East Germany	2	—	1	1	1-2
Eire	6	5	1	—	16-4
England	8	3	3	2	7-7
Finland	4	4	—	—	23-1
France	6	3	—	3	10-8
Georgia	2	2	—	—	7-2
Germany (inc West)	8	1	1	6	4-10
Greece	2	—	1	1	1-3
Holland	7	4	1	2	13-8
Hungary	10	5	1	4	19-13
Iceland	2	2	—	—	9-0
Italy	9	3	3	3	6-5
Luxemburg	2	2	—	—	11-1
Malta	2	2	—	—	7-1
Norway	2	2	—	—	5-2
Poland	2	—	1	1	2-4
Portugal	10	5	2	3	16-9
Romania	2	1	—	1	2-2
Russia	6	1	3	2	8-8
Slovakia	2	1	1	—	1-0
Spain	12	2	4	6	11-20
Switzerland	12	8	2	2	26-11
Wales	2	2	—	—	8-0
Yugoslavia	8	4	1	3	18-11

SUBSTITUTES

The initial use of subs in the mid 1960s to cover for injury has given way to today's more sophisticated tactical chessgame.

The first substitute to take the field in a League game for Celtic was Steve Chalmers. He entered the fray at Dundee on 24 September 1966, and promptly became the first sub to score for the Bhoys in a competitive match – which Celtic won 2-1. The first substitute of all was Willie O'Neill, a full-back who played 86 times for Celtic before moving to Carlisle. He came on at St Mirren in a League Cup encounter on 3 September 1966, which Celtic won 1-0.

During the FA Cup campaign in the glory season of 1966-67, Willie Wallace came on as sub against Elgin City (7-0 to Celtic) and became the club's first substitute to score twice. Only six substitutes were used during that first season. They were Chalmers (twice) Jim Craig, Bobby Lennox, Jim Brogan, O'Neill, Wallace and John Hughes.

The number of subs used had doubled by 1967-68. There were 12: Hughes, Davie Cattanach (three times – one goal), O'Neill (twice), Brogan, Joe McBride (three times), Wallace, Jimmy Quinn (twice – one goal), Bertie Auld (twice – one goal), Chalmers (five times), David Hay, George Connelly and Lou Macari.

The first time Celtic used two substitutes was in the European Cup game at Benfica in November 1969. Harry Hood, who had scored one of Celtic's goals in the 3-0 win at Parkhead, was one, and the other was Connelly. Neither was able to help Celtic overcome Benfica on the night, and the tie was decided on the toss of a coin.

The next time Celtic used two subs was against Kokkola in the 1970 European Cup and the substitutes used were Vic Davidson and Paul Wilson. Wilson scored twice in the 9-0 victory, and thus became the second Celtic player to score twice as a sub. He also scored as a substitute in a 5-1 League Cup win over Dundee during that month.

Hood spent a lot of time on the bench. He came on to the field from a sitting position on 46 occasions, which was surprising for such a cool and skilful striker. Described as the supersub of all time, he came on for Kenny Dalglish at Ibrox in August 1973, scored a goal and set up a late one for Bobby Lennox as Celtic beat Rangers in the League Cup.

George McCluskey was another striker who spent time on the bench during his term at Celtic. He was used as a sub on 32 occasions in League games and was himself substituted in a dozen League encounters between November 1975 and September 1982. He was, however, almost ever present in 1981-82, when he missed only one League game and two in the League Cup (coming on as substitute in one of them). He was the scorer of some fine goals, and was missed following his transfer to Leeds United in the summer of 1983.

In recent years the use of substitutes has increased markedly. In the 1991-92 season for example, Celtic used subs in every League game except one, and in all League Cup, Scottish Cup and UEFA Cup matches. In the three cup competitions, two subs were used on every occasion, while in the League a single sub was used on just eight occasions, with two being used 35 times. The principal players involved were Steve Fulton, Tony Cascarino, Gerry Creaney and Mike Galloway. Fulton, Cascarino and Creaney each came on 14 times, while Galloway made a dozen appearances.

In terms of individual performance, though, the supersub accolade goes to Andy Payton who, on 25 August 1993, came on as a substitute in a League Cup game at Arbroath. He scored three times as Celtic beat the Red Lichties 9-1.

DREAM TEAM 3

After the glory days of the late 1960s, some great players have worn the green and white, but great sides have been relatively few and far between. However, in 1987–88, Celtic produced a Double-winnning team – the first for 11 years.

Goalkeeper   Packy Bonner
Suffered a virus attack to go with his bad back and from time
to time gave way to Allen McKnight, missing a total of 17
games in all. Sadly for the Republic of Ireland man, he also
damaged a hamstring in training shortly before the Scottish
Cup Final.

Right-back   Chris Morris
Signed by Billy McNeill for £100,000 in time for the start of
Celtic's Centenary Season. Had not proved popular at his
previous club, Sheffield Wednesday, but 1987-88 was to be his
year and he was ever-present.

Left-back   Anton Rogan
On the substitutes' bench some of the time, but he made a
significant contribution when he came on for Joe Miller at
Ibrox in March and helped his side to a 2-1 victory. He was
also in the starting line-up for both the Semi-Final and the
Scottish Cup Final, and the two UEFA Cup games against
Borussia Dortmund.

Central defender   Roy Aitken
Wore the Number 4 shirt all season and did an excellent job.

Central defender   **Derek Whyte**

Whyte was a versatile player and mostly wore 5, but seemed equally at home at 6 or 3. Mick McCarthy and Lex Baillie also filled the centre-half position during the course of the season.

Midfielder   **Peter Grant**

The promising midfielder broke his foot playing against St Mirren in April and missed the later stages of the League and Cup battles.

Midfielder   **Billy Stark**

Started his professional career with St Mirren, where he was described as one of the most casual players in the game. He moved to Aberdeen and then Celtic, and early in the season scored the only goal of the first home encounter with Rangers. Joe Miller featured in the Cup Final which Stark missed.

Midfielder   **Paul McStay**

In a class of his own as ever, Celtic's long-serving midfielder missed just one League Cup game all season.

Striker   **Frank McAvennie**
Scored 18 times in 38 games after signing from West Ham in
October. He claimed all four in a League match at Morton,
and both goals in the Cup Final against Dundee United.

Striker   **Andy Walker**
Signed pre-season, he scored two in Celtic's first League game
against Morton. He was almost ever-present in the League
side and scored twice within a minute against Dundee near
the season's end.

Midfielder   **Tommy Burns**
Getting towards the end of his illustrious playing career,
'Twists and Turns' made 23 appearances and scored three
times.

WORST SEASON 3

Rangers won the Premier Division title in 1988–89 and have been winning it ever since. Celtic last won it in 1987–88, but within two years they were to finish in their lowest Premier place up until that time.

In the 1989–90 season it was, once more, the Celts' home record that largely let them down. Home statistics of six wins, six draws and six defeats, with 21 goals scored and 20 conceded, are less than impressive. Celtic were beaten at home by Dundee United, Dunfermline, Rangers, Motherwell, St Mirren and Aberdeen, although at least none of these clubs managed to win twice at Celtic Park.

Celtic also managed only four away wins all season, at Hearts, Dundee, Hibernian and St Mirren, but they did manage to draw eight times on away soil. Packy Bonner was ever-present and, despite the results, only conceded 37 times in the 36 matches played. Chris Morris was mainly at right-back while, from November onwards, Polish captain and £400,000 signing Dariusz Wdowczyk was his counterpart on the left. Lewisham-born Paul Elliott was mainly at centre-half, while the by now ageing Roy Aitken, Derek Whyte and Anton Rogan also featured defensively.

Paul McStay, who missed only one game in all competitions that season, took over the captaincy from Aitken in January. He played a vital role, but scored only two League goals, while midfielder Mike Galloway, a new signing from Hearts for £500,000 in June 1989, scored in his second League outing but netted only once more in the League all season. Another Dariusz – this one Dziekanowski – made his debut in the Number 9 shirt at the start of the season, but proved to be a disappointment. He plundered four of Celtic's five goals in the European Cup Winners' Cup game against Partizan Belgrade, but scored only eight in the League. Tommy Coyne scored seven in the League, and also netted the goal which put Rangers out of the Cup. Andy Walker, who spent much of the season on the subs' bench, scored six, while Joe Miller – also a fairly frequent sub – scored five.

Celtic failed to score in 15 of their 36 League matches. They also failed to win any of the last eight fixtures, notching up four draws and four defeats and scoring just four goals in the process. They finished fifth in the table with 34 points, having both scored and conceded 37 goals. When they lost the Scottish Cup Final on penalties to Aberdeen, there seemed to be something inevitable about it.

1989-90 LEAGUE RECORD

Opponents	Home	Away
Aberdeen	1-0	1-1
Aberdeen	1-3	1-1
Dundee	4-1	3-1
Dundee	1-1	0-0
Dundee United	0-1	2-2
Dundee United	3-0	0-2
Dunfermline Athletic	1-0	0-2
Dunfermline Athletic	0-2	0-0
Hearts	2-1	3-1
Hearts	1-1	0-0
Hibernian	3-1	3-0
Hibernian	1-1	0-1
Motherwell	1-1	0-0
Motherwell	0-1	1-1
Rangers	1-1	0-1
Rangers	0-1	0-3
St Mirren	1-1	0-1
St Mirren	0-3	2-0

PARKHEAD'S ROLL OF HONOUR

1888-89	FA Cup Runners-up
1891-92	Division One Runners-up, FA Cup Winners
1892-93	Division One Champions, FA Cup Runners-up
1893-94	Division One Champions, FA Cup Runners-up
1894-95	Division One Runners-up
1895-96	Division One Champions
1897-98	Division One Champions
1898-99	FA Cup Winners
1899-1900	Division One Runners-up, FA Cup Winners
1900-01	Division One Runners-up, FA Cup Runners-up
1901-02	Division One Runners-up, FA Cup Runners-up
1903-04	FA Cup Winners
1904-05	Division One Champions
1905-06	Division One Champions
1906-07	Division One Champions, FA Cup Winners
1907-0	Division One Champions, FA Cup Winners
1908-09	Division One Champions
1909-10	Division One Champions
1910-11	FA Cup Winners
1911-12	Division One Runners-up, FA Cup Winners
1912-13	Division One Runners-up
1913-14	Division One Champions, FA Cup Winners
1914-15	Division One Champions
1915-16	Division One Champions
1916-17	Division One Champions
1917-18	Division One Runners-up
1918-19	Division One Champions
1919-20	Division One Runners-up
1920-21	Division One Runners-up
1921-22	Division One Champions
1922-23	FA Cup Winners
1924-25	FA Cup Winners
1925-26	Division One Champions, FA Cup Runners-up
1926-27	FA Cup Winners
1927-28	Division One Runners-up, FA Cup Runners-up
1928-29	Division One Runners-up
1930-31	Division One Runners-up, FA Cup Winners
1932-33	FA Cup Winners
1934-35	Division One Runners-up
1935-36	Division One Champions
1936-37	FA Cup Winners
1937-38	Division One Champions
1938-39	Division One Runners-up
1950-51	FA Cup Winners
1953-54	Division A Champions,

	FA Cup Winners
1954-55	Division A Runners-up, FA Cup Runners-up
1955-56	FA Cup Runners-up
1956-57	League Cup Winners
1957-58	League Cup Winners
1960-61	FA Cup Runners-up
1962-63	FA Cup Runners-up
1964-65	FA Cup Winners, League Cup Runners-up
1965-66	Division One Champions, FA Cup Runners-up, League Cup Winners
1966-67	Division One Champions, FA Cup Winners, League Cup Winners, European Cup Winners
1967-68	Division One Champions, League Cup Winners
1968-69	Division One Champions, FA Cup Winners, League Cup Winners
1969-70	Division One Champions, FA Cup Runners-up, League Cup Winners, European Cup Runners-up
1970-71	Division One Champions, FA Cup Winners, League Cup Runners-up
1971-72	Division One Champions, FA Cup Winners, League Cup Runners-up
1972-73	Division One Champions, FA Cup Runners-up, League Cup Runners-up
1973-74	Division One Champions, FA Cup Winners,
	League Cup Runners-up
1974-75	FA Cup Winners, League Cup Winners
1975-76	Premier Division Runners-up, League Cup Runners-up
1976-77	Premier Division Champions, FA Cup Winners, League Cup Runners-up
1977-78	League Cup Runners-up
1978-79	Premier Division Champions
1979-80	Premier Division Runners-up, FA Cup Winners
1980-81	Premier Division Champions
1981-82	Premier Division Champions
1982-83	Premier Division Runners-up, League Cup Winners
1983-84	Premier Division Runners-up, FA Cup Runners-up, League Cup Runners-up
1984-85	Premier Division Runners-up, FA Cup Winners
1985-86	Premier Division Champions
1986-87	Premier Division Runners-up, League Cup Runners-up
1987-88	Premier Division Champions, FA Cup Winners
1988-89	FA Cup Winners
1989-90	FA Cup Runners-up
1990-91	League Cup Runners-up
1994-95	FA Cup Winners, League Cup Runners-up
1995-96	Premier Division Runners-up
1996-97	Premier Division Runners-up
1997-98	League Cup Winners

QUIZ ANSWERS

See page 122-125 for questions.

1.   1888

2.   Cardiff

3.   John Thomson

4.   3-0

5.   Rieper, Larsson and Burley

6.   Robert

7.   Jimmy McStay

8.   Paul McStay

9.   Willie McStay

10.   Gordon Banks

11.   Pierre van Hooijdonk

12.   Charlie Nicholas

13.   790

14.   1959

15.   Murdo MacLeod

16.   Danny McGrain

17.   Manchester United

18.   Pisa

19. Archdeacon

20. Battles

21. Johnny Bonnar

22. 7–1

23. Billy McPhail

24. John, John – and John!

25. John and Tommy

26. Ginger

27. Jimmy McGrory

28. Bolton Wanderers

29. 43

30. Swindon, West Ham, Birmingham, Stoke and Celtic.

31. 1892–93

32. 1987–88

33. Andy Payton

34. Jacki

35. Shuggie

36. Four

37. Dundee United

38. Paul McStay

39. Motherwell

40. 11–0

THE LAST WORD

'Now all the work we have put in this season has been rewarded, and it is very important both for the players and the supporters to see that we can win trophies.'

Wim Jansen following the 3-0 defeat of Dundee United in the 1997 Coca-Cola Cup Final